DEVIL'S ISLAND

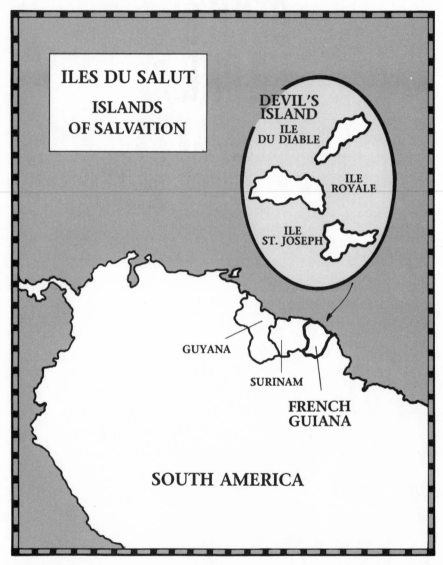

ILES DU SALUT

ISLANDS
OF SALVATION

DEVIL'S
ISLAND
ILE
DU DIABLE

ILE
ROYALE

ILE
ST. JOSEPH

GUYANA

SURINAM

FRENCH
GUIANA

SOUTH AMERICA

Map by J. S. McVey

DEVIL'S ISLAND

Colony of the Damned

Alexander Miles

TEN SPEED PRESS

1⊜ TEN SPEED PRESS
P.O. Box 7123
Berkeley, CA 94707

Cover Design by Fifth Street Design
Typesetting by The Mac Studio
Photograph of chained prisoner reprinted from *HELL BEYOND THE SEAS* by Aage Krarup-Nielsen by permission of the publisher, Vanguard Press, Inc. Copyright © 1936 by Vanguard Press, Inc. & Hearst International. Renewed © 1963 by Vanguard Press, Inc.

Library of Congress Cataloging-in Publication Data
Miles, Alexander.
    Devil's Island.

    Bibliography: p.
    1. Penal colonies—France—History. 2. Penal colonies—French Guiana—History. 3. Penal colonies—French Guiana—Devil's Island—History. I. Title.
HV8956.G8G54   1988   988'.23   88-24838

ISBN 0-89815-275-5 (pbk.)

First Printing, 1988

Manufactured in the United States of America

2 3 4 5 - 92 91

CONTENTS

AUTHOR'S NOTE

The use of French words and phrases has been minimized throughout this book and English terms have been used wherever possible. There are, however, instances where no English equivalent exists for certain legal terms and convict slang. A glossary has been included for this purpose.

GLOSSARY

bagne : prison or penal colonies where sentences of hard labor are served.

doublage : the law that required convicts sentenced to hard labor to reside for a time equal to their sentence in French Guiana.

doudou : native prostitute of French Guiana.

fort-à-bras : strong arm; a particularly rough and domineering prisoner (slang).

libéré : an ex-convict serving under the law of *doublage*.

môme : a young prisoner, usually the passive member of a homosexual relationship (slang).

plan : a suppository used by prisoners to hide money and contraband items (slang).

relégué : a prisoner sent to French Guiana without sentence upon conviction for numerous misdemeanors and required to reside in the colony indefinitely.

tafia : a moonshine rum made from crushed sugar cane and produced in French Guiana for local consumption.

transportation : the practice of sending convict overseas to serve sentences of hard labor.

transporté : a convict serving a term of hard labor in an overseas penal colony.

vieux blanc : old white; an ex-convict who remained in French Guiana after the closing of the penal colony.

INTRODUCTION

The image of Steve McQueen, Clark Gable and Ronald Colman, dressed in striped prison uniforms, darting through snake infested jungle in a desperate attempt to get away from "Devil's Island," is what most likely springs to mind when the place is mentioned. Like any image that goes with a legend, it has some reality to it. It is not clear, though, from this image if the island really existed.

Devil's Island did exist as a prison and does exist today, as a tiny and uninhabited speck off the coast of South America. It became confused with (though it was part of) the entire penal colony of French Guiana when Alfred Dreyfus, the principal character in the Dreyfus Affair, spent five years rotting on the island at the turn of the century.

Since then many films and books have come out with varied, often exaggerated and untrue accounts of what went on in the penal colony. The success of *Papillon* (the book and the film) has only reinforced the ambiguity. Behind all this lies the real story.

The penal colony was nineteenth century France's attempt to kill two birds with one stone. It aimed to rid France of her worst criminals, and at the same time use convict labor to turn Guiana — France's only South American territory — into a self-supporting colony.

The results were mixed. It was extremely successful at ridding France of her worst criminals, as fewer than one in ten survived; they died long before the end of their terms.

But it failed abysmally at turning French Guiana into a self-supporting colony. Virtually every project started during the century of the penal colony's existence was a fiasco, serving only to make the territory even more dependent on French subsidies. Few traces can be found of the efforts of the 70,000 convicts who labored in the jungle and died from a frightening array of tropical diseases. And today, French Guiana is more dependent than ever on handouts from Paris.

The penal colony was another in a series of "development plans" thought up in a Paris office in an attempt to turn the steaming jungle into a model of French civilization. The implementation of this plan was to strangle any hope Guiana had for development and leave the colony in much worse condition than when it began. Several years after the 1954 closure of the penal colony, Robert Vignon, a former prefet (equivalent of colonial governor) of French Guiana, described the devastation like this:

"French Guiana, Cayenne, Devil's Island — such is the inevitable thought process of any Frenchman who thinks, for the first time, about (France's) South American territory. . . . The penitentiary became, for French Guiana, a crown of pain and sorrow which is only slowly being removed."

France has foolishly refused to recognize that her oldest overseas possession's current predicament is neither recent nor easily remedied. Rather, it results from more than three centuries of colonial rule. The problems in today's Cayenne are virtually the same ones faced by residents of that town in 1750. It is clear that any new development plan imposed by Paris will only serve to reinforce this malaise.

One might think that the French Guianese would be strongly inclined toward independence. But many, if not most, suspect that raising a new flag would more than likely create even more dependence on outside forces and leave the fragile Indian population of the interior unprotected from possible abuse. They look to neighboring Surinam with apprehension, as more than 10,000 refugees from there have flooded into French Guiana since 1986 as a result of political and ethnic problems.

And one can hardly view independence for French Guiana as different. It would be pushed on the territory from a Paris bureau, like any of numerous past schemes.

It is easy to assign blame, less so to find solutions that go further than slogan shouting and violence. In French Guiana's isolation, locals have hoped that the events that have touched so much of the Caribbean and Central America in recent years would not touch their hidden corner. And, after some turbulence during the early 1980s, French Guiana has in recent years been calm as a result of massive French subsidies that have raised its standard of living to the highest in South America. The Guiana Space Center in Kourou is Europe's Cape Canaveral, and France has no plans whatsoever of losing it by pushing Guiana toward independence.

Much of the material in this book comes from interviews with former prisoners and civilians in French Guiana and Surinam who were alive during the penal colony era. I have also extensively researched published sources, unpublished reports and documents of the Administration Pénitentiare.

I am deeply indebted to my friends at the old house on Fullum Street in Montreal where I learned to speak French, without which researching and writing this book would have been impossible.

Since 1979, many in French Guiana and abroad have been of tremendous help. To name just a few: the late Jean-Francois Chevallier, Yamille Bragance, Jean Opila, Colin Rickards, Herwig Van de Walle, Michael Gepp and at the last moment Helen Miles and Sy Rayner for their help with De Rudio and Denis Le Her Seznec with the latest information on the Seznec Affair.

Sam Marshall of Mount Kisco, New York, a fellow victim of the "guyanite," was of great assistance during a difficult time while he was engaged in his own biological research of French Guiana's tarantulas.

I would also like to thank Robert Miles for his help in preparing this manuscript and the staff of the New York Public Library. As well, special thanks to Anne-Marie Bruleaux of the French Guiana Archives.

This book is dedicated to my late father, Samuel A. Miles, 1916-1982.

SAINT LAURENT-DU-MARONI 1982

Jungle is on all sides. The thick green wall of the Amazon forest covers the land, the rivers cut through it. Man is the weakest and most vulnerable animal here. For over a thousand miles from the Amazon river the wall covers everything. To the south, the forest continues until it reaches a more temperate zone. To the north, it stops only when the jungle reaches the sea.

Hidden in these backwaters of northeastern South America are small clearings with villages built on river banks, isolated from the rest of the world. They are rarely visited and quickly forgotten, for the jungle surrounds them. Inaccessible from the rest of the continent by road or river, the towns which do appear are like islands.

The Maroni river flows from south to north for 300 miles until it empties into the sea. That the river is an international boundary separating Surinam and French Guiana is hardly noticeable. The villages on both sides look the same. Everyone speaks the same language — Taki-Taki. Bare-breasted women washing clothes on the muddy banks take passing notice of canoes making their way down stream; further up in Indian country there is no washing since there are no clothes.

Twenty-five miles before the river turns to sea, two small towns appear. They face each other from opposite banks and if you are not paying attention you can miss them entirely.

1

On the left is Albina. There are a few houses, a police station and the village disappears into jungle. The first town in Surinam is no more than that. To the west, one hundred miles overland, is Paramaribo, the capital and the only town of any size in the whole country. Yet even there the locals take no notice of their neighbors to the east. Most have never been to French Guiana and most will never find any reason to go there. To the Surinamese it is considered a dead place, too small to take seriously. It is of little surprise that French Guiana is the last colony in South America.

Any native with a canoe will take you over to the French side for a few florins. As the hum of the outboard motor dies down, the waterfront of St. Laurent comes into view. There was a time many years ago when this river bank was well patrolled by the police. But now anyone can walk straight into town without drawing the slightest interest from the officials.

It is not much of a place. It never was to begin with. Four or five rat-infested streets of decaying wooden houses in the old colonial style — some occupied, some deserted. You can see it all in ten minutes.

The whole place, reeks of decay. Old Creole women peer out through the windows of their crumbling structures at any stranger who walks the streets. The open sewers are clogged with filth and drowned rats. Stray dogs paw hungrily at the rodent carcasses. The stench is sickening.

It seems like everything of consequence already took place in St. Laurent years ago. Perhaps an old mining village or railroad town whose doors closed a long while back, leaving the unfortunates who remained to eke out their living as best they can.

None of the young stay. Most are gone by the time they are twenty, some to Cayenne, others to Paris. Anywhere to get away from the misery of St. Laurent.

Those who remain are quite diverse racially. They result from uprootings of peoples from different continents over the centuries. Almost all of the shops are run by Chinese families. The wretched lives they lead in their greasy establishments are passed down from generation to generation. So is their practice of cheating a few pennies out of anyone who can't read or count — half the town's populace.

Blacks, St. Laurent's majority, are quite diverse themselves. They can be found in any circle, from the most successful doctor to the most primitive bare-breasted native. These natives have come recently to St. Laurent, for their home is really up-river. Bush-negroes they are called, since their ancestors escaped into the bush from slavery on the plantations and took up life in the jungle. Now, without the will to return upstream, they camp out in the outskirts of St. Laurent.

There are white men in town, but very few were born and raised here. Most have come in search of fortune that they will never attain. They have come looking for gold and suffer from "gold miners disease," found in every gold camp the world over. Once the miner has a taste of success, no matter how small, the mania gets a hold on him. Repeated failures make him even more determined to try again and again. That is not to say that a man will never find gold in the interior—there is plenty of it there. But to turn a profit is something else entirely. Fifty years ago when quinine was traded gram for gram with gold, the trader who went to the mines left a wealthy man, while the miner shivered from malaria. Today little has changed.

There are other Europeans in St. Laurent. Most are short-term bureaucrats who sit and wait until the end of their contracts—content since they are paid forty percent more for being in an undesirable place. Others are lumber merchants who employ a small army of Brazilian workers, recently arrived and in search of hard currency.

One must not forget the dozen or so Colombians and Dominicans who are St. Laurent's prostitutes. Unwashed, syphilitic and grossly fat, they can all be seen standing nightly in one back alley. In the dim light they resemble figures from a nightmare. A half-hour session seems a veritable ordeal in the filthy rooms they keep a story above. Yet in spite of their appearance, business is brisk on most nights. They are St. Laurent's only available women and they know it.

You may not notice some of the town's very old men. They are certainly far older than anyone else and most of them are white, but gaunt and traumatized in appearance. All are over eighty, and most of them have grotesque fading tattoos on their arms and chests. These men did not come to St. Laurent in search of fortune or in search of anything for that matter, but arrived many years ago chained together on a convict ship. They are the last men of Devil's Island.

The others in town take little notice of them. They have always been in St. Laurent and generations have grown up seeing them. From time to time an occasional outsider may arrive to ask embarrassing questions of them. These attempts are met by an icy silence from the vieux blancs who have no desire to dredge up almost forgotten memories. The most persistent of these outsiders may remain for a week or two, and when they are gone they are quickly forgotten by the town's inhabitants.

There was a time, perhaps twenty years back, that the hope of making a few francs would impel these old men to talk with the strangers who came from nowhere to this end-of-the-world colony. Now they have reached the age where they have no need for money and want to be left alone. And over the years, the visitors became less and less frequent.

Off the main street and down a dirt path choked with weeds and strewn with garbage, is a small wooden house. It is midday and the shutters are closed. Siesta is the one activity taken seriously by residents of St. Laurent. There is no one about on the streets. No one stirs.

It looks like the outside of the house hasn't been painted in twenty years. Fading white-wash exposes the raw wood and the corrugated iron roof is orange from rust. A lizard scurries from beneath the concrete blocks used as steps into the house.

The silence breaks as an old transistor radio crackles into life from within the house. It's hard to hear. The reception is not good today and the announcer's voice fades in and out. The broadcast is coming from Cayenne some two hundred miles away on French Guiana's only radio station. When the radio was new, Brazilian broadcasts came in clearly but now even Cayenne comes in badly.

There is a beep and the noon weather report comes on, followed by international news piped in form Paris. The report begins by giving a forecast that is good 300 days a year in French Guiana: Eighty-five degrees and ninety-five percent humidity, with rain in the afternoon and evening.

There is a pause. A second, even more distant, voice comes on. The announcer reports the measures taken in Warsaw after the arrest of Lech Walesa and the imposition of martial law in Poland two days before. As the broadcast continues other voices are heard, this time coming from inside the house. The news is punctuated by a series a gruff articulations.

"Heuh, les salauds!" a deep voice cackles when the announcer tells of the dusk to dawn curfew being imposed.

"C'est toujours pareil!" a second voice joins in, not as deep as the first, his French is spoken with a Flemish accent.

"Do you think they are going to do the same thing over there as they did in Prague a few years back?" the second voice asks the first.

"I don't think so," the first voice replies. "I think they're too afraid of what Reagan might do!"

The radio is turned off, and the heavily tattooed eighty-nine-year-old figure of Lucien Bellouard reaches for his pack of 'National' brand cigarettes. He extracts one and inserts it carefully into a bamboo holder. At less than two francs a pack they crumble easily.

The man with the Flemish accent is eighty-two-year-old Henri Bauve. The two men now sit in silence for a while, reflecting on the news. After a few minutes they discuss their upcoming trip to Cayenne. They are going there the following week to see the ophthalmologist who will remove the cataracts that have developed in the eyes of both men.

For Lucien Bellouard, it will be a trip to a new town. Despite the fact that he has been in French Guiana for over fifty years, he has never been to Cayenne.

Both men are understandably nervous about the trip. "A blind man might as well make the sign of the cross," Lucien Bellouard remarks. "It's worse than being dead," Henri Bauve agrees. And after sixty years in French Guiana he knows what he's talking about.

Since their release from prison over thirty years ago, both have done the best they could. They had good trades, so surviving in the easy pace of French Guiana was not that difficult. But the time between their release and the retirement brought on by their advancing years was short. That and years before arriving in French Guiana constitute their lives. What went on during their years of imprisonment cannot be described by either of them as "life." They were able to retire on a small government pension—and that is enough.

Both men could have gone back to France when they were released, but they decided to remain in French Guiana.

"In 1932, I cut all ties with my family," Lucien Bellouard recalls. "I wrote to them and told them to consider me as if I were dead and never to write to me again. I thought that was the best thing to do and since then I've heard nothing from them.

"Seeing that I was sentenced to life imprisonment, what was the point in returning to France? The identity papers they gave us upon release from prison would have prevented me from working. On it was the whole story, where, why and when I was convicted. With papers like that nobody in France would have given me a job. It wasn't that they closed the bagne for any humanitarian reason—not in the least. Far from it! They closed the gates and kicked us out only because it cost them too much to keep us. That's the only reason."

For Henri Bauve, it was much the same. "When I went on trial, my court-appointed lawyer argued that I was seventeen when I committed my offence and couldn't be tried as an adult." Even sixty years later, he is reluctant to divulge the reasons for his imprisonment; the pain is as heavy today as it was then.

"The judge interrupted my lawyer and said that though I was seventeen at the time, I was now eighteen. I was sentenced to life imprisonment, but my brother was guillotined, for it was he who actually committed the murder. He had no choice since he would have been killed the next day if he hadn't killed the man."

Lucien Bellouard was ten years older than Henri Bauve when he arrived in le bagne in 1929.

"I was in one of the African battalions during the entire First World War. Always in the desert, we marched at night and slept during the day on account of the heat.

"After the war I returned to France. I was living in a village fifty kilometers from Rennes, and there I had a problem with one of the guys who worked at the ship repair yard in the nearby port. I was taking my meals at a certain hotel and these guys from the port came in. They were very drunk, as they had just finished one of their big jobs. Little by little they started to get rowdy, and began to tear the place up.

"The owner of this hotel was a good friend of mine, I had known him since I was a kid. I couldn't let these guys destroy the place, so I began punching one of them. The owner joined in, and we quickly kicked them out. The fight was over.

"I was working evenings at a construction site and later that night I left to go to work. When you leave a well-lit building, and go onto a dark road, you are completely blinded; you can't see anything. I felt a knife cutting the back of my neck. From the shock, I turned around and saw that it was the guy from earlier in evening. I stumbled back to the hotel and they brought me to the hospital.

"My spinal cord was grazed by the attack, but not severed. If it had been, I would have been dead. From my bed I decided to get even; so after nineteen days, I signed myself out. I knew that if a person stayed in the hospital for more than twenty days, his assailant could be charged with attempted murder and sent to another city at a higher court for trial. He would be out of reach.

"I still had ten metal stitches in my neck and on each side there was a straw that let the fluid drain. The doctor was against releasing me, but I was able to convince him to let me out. He made me sign a document that absolved him of all responsibility.

"I left the hospital and was treated by a doctor in my village. The police came to see me, for they had arrested the man who attacked me.

"I did everything possible to have the man released. The whole thing was tried in a lower court and the man was acquitted.

"When I recovered I went back to work, and on Sundays played accordion in an orchestra. Several months later, I was playing in a dance hall. The place was full, since it was the autumn ball. While playing I noticed a familiar face in the crowd. All of the sudden, I realized that it was the guy who had attacked me. I was taken completely by surprise, and even missed a note or two. The others in the orchestra probably understood what had happened, but they kept on playing. Finally it hit me. I couldn't just let the guy walk away.

"After we finished the piece, I left the dance hall quietly. As soon as I got outside, I ran as fast as I could to my room and got my revolver, a 7.65.

"When night fell, the guy left the dance hall and I followed him. When I found that he was alone I stopped him, aimed the gun and fired one shot.

"I was arrested later on and the prosecutor understood everything. He said, 'You wanted him out of jail so you could go after him yourself. That's premeditation!'

"I was sentenced to life at hard labor and arrived in St. Laurent in 1929. Next week I'm going to Cayenne for the first time."*

The sound of raindrops falling on the iron roof can be heard as another French Guiana afternoon turns into a downpour. Drops pour in from above. There's nothing to do now. Even after a lifetime in St. Laurent, the ferocity of the equatorial deluge disturbs the two men.

---

* Jean-Claude Michelot also met Henri Bauve and Lucien Bellouard and described his encounter with them in *La Guillotine seche*.

The radio is turned on again. Their eyesight failing, it is now their only link with the outside world. In the distance, an outboard motor gets louder as it approaches the French bank of the river. The two men sit and listen to the radio.

A new report announces a bank robbery in the south of France. Their expressions change, and they analyse the crime as two bankers might discuss the midday stock report. The logistics of the operation and the dynamiting of the vault are of special interest, and they hang on to every word.

When the rain stops, the shutters are opened and the residents of St. Laurent take to the streets. Surveying the scene from inside the house, the two men can see quite well now, for it is only in dim light that their vision is reduced to near blindness. Teenage girls in tight-fitting jeans walk by. Both smile, for even at their age they can still admire a pretty girl.

Looking at the garbage that litters the street, Henri Bauve remarks how different it was years ago. "When I arrived here in 1921, this was the cleanest town in South America. You couldn't find a cigarette butt on any street. They were all picked up by the libérés who rerolled them. A whole crew of convicts would be sent out to clean up a piece of paper that had fallen to the ground. If anyone's dog ran off, that was just too bad. The strays that wandered into the libéré village would be pounced on. Hungry men are hungry men!"

Why have Henri Bauve and Lucien Bellouard lived so long? Why are they still alive when their contemporaries are long dead, from the police to the prosecutors to their fellow prisoners? Why are they still alive, thirty–five years after an embarrassed French government closed the prison gates and hoped that the last of these broken men would be forgotten?

The answer is not clear. Yet their longevity perhaps tells the whole story of the most infamous prison the world has known: Above all else, you must survive!

Henri Bauve and Lucien Bellouard have survived, and so has the penal colony known as Devil's Island. More than three decades after its closing, the bagne is still alive on every street and in every alleyway in French Guiana. And it will live on, long after these last men have died, for the stamp of the penal colony has been burned indelibly into the land.

THE MAKING OF A PENAL COLONY

Long before the arrival of the first Europeans, the Indians of what is now French Guiana hunted for sea turtles along the coastline. Villages dotted the rivers and the Indians travelled between them in their dugout canoes. As the first explorers arrived, the Indians retreated into the hidden jungle to observe them from a more secure vantage point.

The first ships contained their share of merciless prospectors and religious fanatics. The steaming jungle looked uninviting, but the gold had to be found and the Indians converted or killed. It is known that Guiana was visited by some of these boats before the beginning of the seventeenth century.

In 1595, Sir Walter Raleigh published *The Discovery of the Large, Rich and Beautiful Empire of Guiana*. The book told of the legend of El Dorado and the area caught the attention of Europe. All the major powers wanted their share of El Dorado's treasure and they began to scramble to obtain it. Spanish and English explorers came first. But the French were also keenly interested.

Under the leadership of Henri IV, the gentleman explorer Daniel de la Ravardiere, Lord of Touche, was sent to Guiana to make a report to the King on the region's potential. He left Le Havre in January of 1604, and returned to France in August of that year. While he had not found El

Dorado — and doubted its existence — he found the region to be quite fascinating, and recommended settlement to the king.

The colonial drive to Guiana now started. The first convoy of French settlers of the Rouen Commercial Company left France in 1626, and twenty-six of them started settlement in the village of Sinnamary. Later some of these settlers joined with new arrivals to settle an island which soon became known as Cayenne. The Rouen company obtained exclusive trade right for the isolated region. A village and fort called Ceperou was constructed in Cayenne, and several other settlements began on the banks of the Maroni river.

But the Rouen Commercial Company was not the only French concern to be hit with "Guiana fever." Several officers from the first settlement ship returned to France and came into contact with Poncet, Lord of Britigny.

Poncet was filled with stories of the savage beauty of Guiana by the officers, and wanted to see Guiana and settle it if possible. Under his leadership, a convoy was assembled and he left France for Guiana with the titles of governor and lieutenant general of the king.

But his convoy was badly assembled. Instead of the farmers and laborers who would be needed to undertake any kind of colonial endeavor, the men who went were almost all soldiers, enticed by stories of golden cities and native women.

Poncet's expedition left France in September of 1643 and reached Cayenne by November. Within hours of arrival, Poncet's behavior confirmed earlier rumours of his insanity. The slightest infraction of his rule was cause for severe punishment, and when several of his officers conspired to overthrow him, they were thrown into a makeshift prison next to a malarial swamp.

A list of 140 articles was drawn up by Poncet, clearly the work of a madman. Blasphemy was punished by having one's tongue cut out with a red hot iron. Anyone who struck the loyal few of Poncet were to have their hands cut off.

Eight innocent men were rounded up and put in jail. Each morning Poncet interrogated them, demanding a full account of their previous night's dream. If their dreams were not to his liking, the unfortunate was branded on the forehead with Poncet's initials.

The Indians were especially mistreated by Poncet, and soon plotted revenge. They waited for the time when Poncet went into the outlying jungle area on an exploration trip and attacked. Completely at home in the jungle, the Indians massacred Poncet and those who accompanied him.

It did not stop there. Fort Ceperou was raided and fell to the Indians. A few of the settlers escaped into the jungle and were rescued by an offshore boat, but for most who were trapped in the fort death came slowly. As rumor had it, they were eaten as steaks by the Indians.

Cayenne lay empty of settlers until 1656, when Guerin Spranger and sixty other Dutch Jews drifted into Guiana after being thrown out of Brazil on religious grounds. Mostly traders by profession, they were accompanied by an even larger number of black slaves. Spranger came to an understanding with the Indians immediately and began to create a small but prosperous colony. Other Jews from Brazil followed, and this new Dutch colony began to produce and export sugar, where the previous French colonists had produced only murder and conspiracy. For several years, the colony was ignored by the rest of the world.

But France still had her eyes on Guiana and in 1663, an expedition was organized to remove the Dutch from Cayenne. Twelve hundred men arrived the following year and

Spranger, faced with almost certain military defeat if he resisted, surrendered to the French. He was accorded safe passage to Surinam, the new English colony to the west.

The new French regime was delighted to find a well-organized colony. The slaves brought by the Dutch were working in the fields cutting cane and, following Spranger's example, the new governor made a non-aggression treaty with the Indians. The Indians would be let alone if they left the island of Cayenne and aided the French in capturing runaway slaves. The Indians agreed to this at once.

During the next century, Guiana changed hands four times; over to the English, back to the Dutch and once again to French rule. The problem of populating the colony, however, was never solved.

In Europe, the sinister reputation of Guiana was just a rumor handed down from the few who had returned to France. The deathly reputation of the colony became known throughout France in 1763, with the nightmare expedition of the Duc de Choiseul.

The French Empire was in trouble; in that year the Treaty of Paris switched Canada and Cape Breton as well as Louisiana west of the Mississippi from French to English control. Most of the Caribbean was lost to the British as well, as England began to control more and more of the Americas after their victory in the Seven Years' War.

With his empire waning, Louis XV focused on Guiana as an area where the colonial drive could be re-established. Since slave rebellions had become frequent, it was decided to send only white Frenchmen. The coastal hamlet of Kourou was chosen and within several months 14,000 settlers arrived.

From the very first day disasters plagued these new colonists. Nothing had been prepared for their arrival, and, ignorant of the climate and terrified of the jungle, they huddled in clumsily built shelters near the Kourou river. Epidemics raged throughout the camps. The bodies piled up so quickly that burial gave way to tossing the dead into the sea. In all, over 10,000 died during the first two years, and those who survived took refuge off the coast of Guiana on three islands they called *Iles du Salut* (Salvation Islands). And this was their salvation, since malaria and typhoid occurred less frequently there. The climate was healthier than the swamps of Kourou and the fish were abundant. When a few of the survivors returned to France in later years, the horror of the disaster became known to the French public and many now felt that Guiana was in some way cursed.

At the time of the French revolution in 1789, there were fifteen hundred whites, ten thousand slaves and five hundred freed blacks in the colony. The revolution brought freedom to the slaves and many headed for the interior where they set up villages. Escaped slaves joined them, and they recreated their native Africa in the South American jungle.

In France, where the new regime had produced many undesirables, many who had been spared the guillotine were now rotting in French prisons. Guiana, with its horrible reputation, seemed an ideal location for opponents of the new order. The prisoners were rounded up, but not deported for several years, as France was again at war with England and maritime lanes were blocked. In 1795 the first convoy arrived with such notables as Collot d'Herbois and Billaud-Varenne, and in 1798, more than three hundred other political exiles were sent. Most of the exiles were priests who refused to take an oath of obedience, and they died rapidly from tropical diseases. Seven hundred men were deported to Guiana, but the plan to settle the colony with exiles didn't work; most of the prisoners were in such bad health that they couldn't work.

Revolutionary fervor died quickly at the turn of the century, and Consul Victor Hugues re-established slavery, for emancipation left the colonies without needed manpower. French Guiana again returned to the hands of foreign powers — a British-Portuguese occupation in 1807 lasted eight years — and when control was returned to France, there were increasing calls to abolish slavery for a second time. In Guiana, Anne-Marie Javouhey pressed for abolition and started a center for freed slaves near the Mana river. Prosperity came slowly to the settlement, but eventually Mana became self-sufficient; with the support of Victor Schoelcher came complete emancipation in 1848.

The end of slave labor created a crisis in Martinique and Guadaloupe, and the great sugar estates rapidly declined. The European powers, who less than fifty years before were battling furiously for territory and influence in the Americas, had moved on to Africa and Asia. They were still the rule of law in most of the Caribbean but the action now lay elsewhere.

In the midst of all this, French Guiana was more isolated than ever. Still virtually an island — no roads had been constructed to link the coastal settlements together — the few plantations that had been developed closed and were quickly overrun with jungle. Former slaves took to the jungle or hung out in coastal towns where they refused to work the land. Cayenne, which now held the entire European population, was bewildered and the general concensus there held that *in Paris there must be a solution to all this!*

From Paris came an idea. Why not send indentured Chinese laborers to Guiana? They would certainly be eager to come to the colony and would probably want to remain in Guiana after their contracts expired. Between 1848 and 1851, several boatloads of Orientals arrived, but it was apparent from the beginning they had no inclination to work the land. When their contracts expired, most headed for Cayenne and set up small retail shops. Most of the plantation owners joined them, and the plantations disappeared completely in the dense vegetation.

After two centuries of French rule, Guiana was little more than virgin jungle dotted here and there with coastal villages. France had absolutely nothing to show for its investment, and again residents of Cayenne looked to Paris for a solution.

In 1852, Louis Napoleon III fixed upon a solution to France's crime problem. More than 6,000 prisoners bloated the naval budget, since they were kept in floating prisons off the coast of France. Why not send these men to Guiana — this would rid France of her undesirables, and at the same time help develop the colony. To ensure that they would remain after their sentence, Napoleon III decided to require the convicts to reside in Guiana as "free men" for a period equal to their original sentence. He figured that most of the men would marry local women upon release — better still, female convicts could be sent there as well.

This seemed to be the perfect plan, at least on paper; so later that year, the first shipment of convicts arrived in Guiana.

In the past, a man condemned to the tortuous life on the offshore galleys could escape that fate by paying a Turkish volunteer to take his place. There was never a shortage of volunteers, but few had the means to pay a Turk to carry out the years of rowing he had been condemned to. Along with convicts and Turks were slaves — any Moslem, or publicly declared Protestant was fated to spend the rest of his days in these floating prisons.

Advances in naval design, however, made these galleys obsolete. More efficient sailing vessels didn't need convicts to provide propulsion, and the era of the galley slave came to an end.

From medieval times the galleys had been the cream of the French naval arsenal, but disposing of the convicts and boats would be a problem. In 1748, the galleys (which had been an independent military force) were turned over to the Navy. Though reluctant to take over these primitive vessels, the Navy acquiesced and found itself with 4,000 convicts, most in a deplorable state. All but the Turks had been branded by a hot iron with the initials "G.A.L.," not so much as a punishment but as a means of identity. The rare galley convict who managed to escape could never deny his past.

The officers and crew of the galleys posed much less of a problem for the Navy. These excellent sailors became reinforcements and performed well after they learned the vocabulary of the modern Navy. Communication in the galleys was comprised of an archaic maritime jargon, out of use for centuries.

The men who had endured years in the galleys were now land-locked and chained together, to endure more years of hard labor in the naval ports of Marseille and Toulon. The red-hot iron brand now bore the initials "T.F." for *travaux forcé* (forced labor). In these ports the work was as arduous as in the rowing fatigues. Carrying heavy beams of wood for shipbuilding was a task reserved for those in the disciplinary battalion, as was pumping out the dry docks. A malfunction in the primitive pump system would mean certain drowning for the men working below.

The bagnes emerged slowly in the French port cities of Rochefort, Toulon and Brest. The human cargo which had been an unwelcome gift to the Navy was considered in terms of francs and days of labor rather than men. Nothing had been prepared in the ports to house these convicts, and their transport was left in the hands of a civilian contractor. Profit to the contractor depended on giving out the most meager rations and many fatalities occurred while the prisoners were marched from Bicetre to the southern ports. When they passed through provincial towns en route, the entire populace came out to look and jeer. The convicts would try to hide their faces from the townsmen, out of shame to some extent, but mostly to hide their identities in case they should have the good fortune to escape in the months or years to come.

The convicts built their own prisons. Brest was constructed in 1750 to accommodate five hundred convicts and its design was noted for the underground passages and catwalks that permitted the guards almost total surveillance over the prisoners. Built on the edge of the town where the canal emptied into the sea, its sanitary conditions were atrocious. During high tide the canals filled, cleaning the sewers and diluting the sewage that emptied into the sea. But at low tide the canals dried up, leaving the residue from the homes and sewers of Brest. The stench permeated the convicts' cells and sent the men choking and gasping for fresh air. Disease spread quickly throughout the prison and the death rate mounted.

The bagne at Rochefort had the highest mortality rate. Constructed in 1766, it never held more than five hundred convicts despite the constant new arrivals. It was located next to a swamp and typhus and malaria raged through the prison, sparing few.

Conditions in these prisons, though having the effect of eliminating criminals from the streets, didn't produce the desired results. The ever-visible structures of the prisons were a constant reminder of their expense, and those who survived would be back one day on the streets to commit new crimes. Their contribution to the Navy was questionable due the the the high cost of guarding and feeding them.

Not that they were well fed! At the beginning of the nineteenth century, the daily ration consisted of dried beans and a kilo of bread, with occasional supplements of wine and cider. In 1819, the prison authorities, faced with a soaring death rate and low productivity, asked for an increase in the food allotment. It wasn't until fifteen years later that their proposals were put into effect. In 1836, the convicts ate meat for the first time in the history of the bagne, yet even this proved insufficient since much of the food was pilfered and sold on the open market.

To the relief of prisoners who received funds from outside, the guards permitted them to buy food from local grocers. From inside the prison walls, convicts could buy anything available in town. For less fortunate men without funds, survival on beans and sea biscuits was a guarantee of scurvy and death.

Even more appalling to the French government was the prospect of reintegrating convicts who finished their terms. The ex-convicts were issued a yellow passport upon release, a type of ex-convict identity paper. In it was the man's entire criminal history; few prospective employers would hire such a man. Soon, he would be back to his old criminal habits and back behind bars.

The idea of transporting French criminals overseas was not new. Rochefort, Toulon and Brest were too close for France's really depraved criminals. To rid France of her undesirables and build up her colonies by sending them across the world was tempting in light of English deportations to Australia.

Louis Napoleon III's fascination with Australia and his disgust with Rochefort, Brest and Toulon made it certain that Guiana would be the eventual site of a penal colony.

Other colonies had been considered, but Guiana seemed ideal since it was closer than most of the Pacific colonies, and much was still expected of the territory.

Louis Napoleon had his feelers out in French Guiana at the time. In a report (the document gives no indication of who the official was) dated December 25, 1851: "The establishment of a penal colony isn't a secondary matter; for France it's a question of security; for the penal administration a question of humanity, for the convicts themselves a question of relative well-being."

Guiana was pushed as *the* solution for France's criminal justice and colonial problem. It would satisfy conservatives by getting rid of the convicts. It would satisfy commercial interests by opening up French Amazonia. The liberals would like it as well, since there was a humanitarian argument behind the penal colony — fewer death sentences and better conditions than in French jails.

If anyone pointed out the previous attempts to colonize Guiana and the failures and fiascoes they produced, Louis Napoleon didn't seem the least bit concerned. At last France would be rid of those wretched convicts!

THE EARLY YEARS

Louis Napoleon III had a clear idea of what type of prison Guiana would be, and few illusions of the character of men and women to be sent there. Under his direction, a list of eleven regulations were drawn up. These would form the basis of the rules the convicts would live under.

The first ten dealt with punishments to be meted out to those who broke the law. The last, added perhaps as an afterthought, provided for Guiana to be developed by convict labor.

ARTICLE I. Future sentences of hard labor will be served in establishments created by decree of the Emperor. They will be carried out in one of the colonial territories, except Algeria.

ARTICLE II. These convicts will be employed in the most difficult aspects and tasks of colonization and at other public works.

ARTICLE III. They can for reasons of security or punishment, be chained together two by two or attached to a ball and chain.

ARTICLE IV. Women sentenced to hard labor can be shipped as well to one of these colonial territories. They will be kept separate from the male prisoners and be put to work at tasks giving consideration to their age and sex.

ARTICLE V. Only those aged sixty or less will be sentenced to hard labor. Individuals sixty and above will be given normal prison sentences, to be served in France or in the location of conviction.

ARTICLE VI. All convicts sentenced to less than eight years will reside after their sentence is completed for a period equal to their sentence in the colonial territory.

If the sentence is eight years or more, the convict will reside for the rest of his or her life in the colonial territory.

By authorization of the Governor of the colony, a libéré can be permitted to leave the colony for a limited period of time. In no case, however, can a libéré be authorized to enter into France.

In case of pardon, a libéré can be excused from doublage by a special letter of decree.

ARTICLE VII. A convict sentenced to hard labor, convicted of escape, will be sentenced to no less than two and no more than five additional years of hard labor.

This sentence cannot be served concurrently with the original sentence.

Convicts sentenced to hard labor for life, convicted of escape, will be sentenced to wear double chains for no less than two and no more than five years.

ARTICLE VIII. A libéré, who under the terms of Article VI leaves the colony without authorization or who overstays a granted authorization to leave the colony, will be sentenced to no less than one and no less than three years of hard labor.

ARTICLE IX. In the case of apprehension during an escape or in violation of infraction of Article VI, the pronouncement of sentence will be made by either a tribunal to be described in the next article or by the original court of condemnation.

ARTICLE X. Infractions mentioned in articles VII and VIII and all other crimes and infractions committed by convicts and libérés will be judged by a special maritime tribunal to be created in the colony.

Until the creation of this tribunal, all convicts and libérés will be judged by the first military court of the colony, to be comprised of two naval officers.

Previous sentences are to be continued by the military court.

ARTICLE XI. Convicts of both sexes, judged to be rehabilitated by acts of work, good behavior and repentance can be permitted to obtain:

1-the authorization to work under conditions determined by the penal administration for inhabitants of the colony or for the local administration.

2-a plot of land and materials to cultivate it. The convict can be made permanent owner when sentence is completed.

The sailing ship *Allier* arrived in Cayenne with three hundred and one convicts who left France on March 27th, 1852. As with the expedition to Kourou a century before, nothing had been prepared for the first convoy of prisoners to Guiana.

Ile Royale was chosen as the first site for the prison colony. The convicts quickly cleared the overgrown vegetation and there seemed to be a feeling of euphoria among the men. Perhaps they would be able to remake their lives in Guiana. The change from the stone prisons of France to Royale, and the possibility of gaining a small plot of land on the mainland encouraged them.

On the mainland at Remire, in the vicinity of Cayenne, a series of huts were constructed to lodge the new arrivals. By the end of the year over 2,000 convicts from France were in Guiana, and were expected to develop and open up the interior of the colony.

In an uninhabited and almost unexplored area of the coastal Guiana forest near the Brazilian border, stood a small hill. Its proximity to the swamps made it seem like a small island surrounded by a never-ending breeding ground for malarial mosquitos. Here at Montagne d'Argent, the first jungle camp of French Guiana's penal colony came into use. At its opening in 1853, more than three hundred convicts began to create a settlement. They were lodged in tents and ate out of doors. No thought had been given to sanitation.

Within the first year, after the fevers had taken hold of the men and the open sores from working in the swamps infected them, half were dead. The misery which this kind of hell engendered drove many to suicide and the discipline, which was originally intended to allow them a small amount of freedom, rapidly resorted back to that of the rowing galleys.

The actual horror of the convict settlements had set in.

Philipe Fournier, a naval officer detached to the camp during his tour of service in Guiana, wrote to a colleague in France describing Christmas Eve, 1853. "Christmas Eve we formed a firing squad to execute a convict who killed a guard. I wanted to go watch, but couldn't since I was weak from an attack of fever. The guard was a father of five children."

Even after the disaster of the first year of Montagne d'Argent, it took fifteen years for the authorities to close the camp and let the jungle obliterate all traces of it.

On the Oyapock river, at what is now the border with Brazil, a camp created at the same time of Montagne d'Argent killed even more men. St. George's swamps were situated below sea level and had no height for cooling breezes to blow. Fever and suicides killed off half the original one hundred and eighty convicts in the first five months of its operation.

Other camps in the western region of the colony were established, all with the same disastrous results. In 1855, settlements near the hamlets of St. Marie and St. Augustine opened and closed killing or debilitating all who were sent there.

It became clear to the penitentiary administration that another area of the colony would have to be used if any of the convicts were to survive to contribute to French Guiana's development. The wholesale slaughter at St. George and Montagne d'Argent couldn't go on much longer. If it had been the intention to kill off convicts so quickly, a guillotine rather than a forest camp would be quicker and cleaner for everyone involved. Kourou and the surrounding jungle camps were faring no better. An epidemic of yellow fever and floods were producing a death rate near that of St. George.

The first five years of the penal colony had done nothing for Guiana. The stories told by the guards and soldiers returning to France from their tours of duty reinforced French Guiana's hideous reputation. By 1856, with the ships from France still arriving, only 3,600 of the 8,600 convicts sent to Guiana were still alive. Montagne d'Argent alone claimed six hundred lives.

What was to become the center of the penal colony started out as an Indian village twenty-five miles from the sea on the Maroni river. The nomadic Galibis abandoned the area taking their one hundred and fifty villagers to another spot along the teeming river.

In 1857, after a rapid study of the region, the tiny village of Saint-Laurent du Maroni opened for convict use. Several jungle camps toward the village of Mana opened and were just as quickly depleted by the same illnesses that had plagued the other establishments. The convicts, forced to work clearing the jungle with only a machete and an axe while shivering from malaria, dropped like flies.

The Indians who remained in St. Laurent stood by in bewilderment as the convicts, prodded by French soldiers and Arab overseers, toiled away at futile tasks. No one thought to ask the Indians what they thought of the European system—they headed further away from the settlements and deeper into the jungle.

Later that year, St. Laurent was chosen as the site for a "penal city." Though it wasn't clear at the time, the decision to group most of the prisoners in one area effectively halted the hopes of using convict labor to open up the colony. Throughout the next eighty years various governors did start small camps in various jungle locations. But from its conception, St. Laurent was the capital of the bagne where two-thirds of the convict population would serve their time. Those not in St. Laurent pined away on the Iles du Salut and at Cayenne, leaving the interior unsettled and largely unexplored.

By 1860, St. Laurent and its surrounding area was designated as a special region for use exclusively as a penal colony. St. Laurent was to be the center of a small agricultural community fed by the forest camps in the outlying region. But that same year, a malaria epidemic put the whole project in jeopardy.

In 1867, France decided to suspend the transport of convicts to Guiana. Fifteen years after the bagne was opened and thousands of deaths later, the colony was not much different from when it had begun. Already ten governors had arrived and then been called back to France — each having had a scheme to make French Guiana the envy of the Americas.

For the next fifteen years, European prisoners sentenced to hard labor were sent to New Caledonia in the French Pacific. When the transports to Guiana resumed in 1883, the camps near St. Laurent had all but disappeared in the dense vegetation.

Construction now began to create a village whose only function was to be a giant prison. Homes for guards and officials went up, as well as a police station and a dock for the Navy. A hospital and barracks for the prisoners were begun, and St. Laurent became the center of the penal colony — both in number of convicts and in importance to the prison administration. In France, the name 'Cayenne' became confused with the entire penal colony by the popular press. In America it was dubbed 'Devil's Island.'

In 1880, an entire region covering 180,000 hectares was designated a 'Penitentiary Territory.' One hundred kilometers long and twenty kilometers wide, it was no longer under the direct jurisdiction of the colony of French Guiana. Its capital, St. Laurent, was run by a seven-member council, consisting of the highest ranking military officer in the area, the director of the penal administration, a justice of the peace and four other members appointed by the governor.

St. Laurent began to emerge as one of the most bizarre small towns in South America. Its population at the turn of the century stood at 5,000, of which 2,000 were convicts under sentence, and another 1,000 prisoners and libérés granted plots of land on the outskirts of town.

The civilians not connected with the penal colony were a diverse lot; most were gold miners staying in town between trips, Chinese shopkeepers and a few Creoles. Apart from these few civilians, everyone who was not a convict was an employee of the penal administration in one capacity or another.

St. Laurent was a model of colonial architectural design. The homes and offices were solidly built with long verandas flanking the outside; there, the guards drank a midday punch or evening aperitif served by convict houseboys. The stifling heat was reduced by the design of these homes which took advantage of the wind and breezes.

The wide streets and handsome homes gave an impression of grandeur; immaculately kept gardens fronted and separated the structures. Not a weed was to be seen, nor any rubbish found in the street. It was all gathered up and disposed of by convicts dressed in pajama-like cotton swim suits with vertical red stripes and straw hats.

In the streets, the only sign of misery was wandering libérés dressed in rags and pushing wheelbarrows. Proud officials dressed in immaculate colonial uniforms and sun helmets passed the ragamuffin ex-convicts without casting the slightest glance in their direction. White women, followed by young convicts carrying their packages, could be seen leaving the vegetable market.

At midday when the heat became unbearable, a long line of pajama-clad figures made their way to the center of town where the penitentiary stood. From the outside, the prison looked imposing — it was sided by concrete walls thirty feet in height. The main gate was guarded by officers with white holsters strapped around their waists, assisted by Arab turnkeys. The turnkeys were dressed exactly like the convicts, but wore a small patch on their sleeves in the form of two crossed keys that identified them to the guards as trusties.

As the convicts reached the main gate, their arms raised mechanically as they were frisked by the Arabs. After the rapid search they entered the compound.

The inside of the camp consisted of sixteen concrete barracks, resembling an army compound rather than a prison. A long veranda flanked the outside so the guards could patrol the barracks without entering.

Inside the barracks one could walk the entire length of the structure. On both sides were long, elevated wooden planks, and as many as eighty men slept on each of these boards (during the last years of the penal colony, the planks were replaced by hammocks). Before 1926, an iron bar ran the length of the plank, and prisoners were bolted to it by their feet at night. In the middle of the barrack a small oil lamp was suspended from the ceiling, giving off just enough light to keep the barrack from total darkness at night.

At the head of each plank were small wooden cubbies where each man kept his personal possessions — a spare shirt, small oil lamps made from empty condensed milk tins, books — anything that wasn't against prison regulations. When the convicts were outside the barracks during the day, a keeper (usually an old convict) stayed inside to clean the latrine buckets and make sure that nothing was stolen.

Theft was not a great problem among the transportés. Lucien Bellouard spent years at St. Laurent and never felt the least bit worried about his worldly goods. "In St. Laurent among the transportés, we were sometimes one hundred and fifty in the barracks. You could have left anything there — no man would touch another's gear. If someone wanted a cigarette he would never just take it from another man, he would ask first. Meanwhile in St. Jean among the relégués, there was theft all the time. It was disgusting."

Behind the *Camp de la Transportation* was a hospital containing eight two-story white-washed units. They served as the medical facility for all the camps in the vicinity of St. Laurent. Further along toward the river was the dock that served as the disembarkation point for newly arrived convicts from France and North Africa.

During a lenient regime of the penal administration, life for convicts in St. Laurent was bearable. The municipal services of the town employed convict labor and if a man knew a needed trade and kept a cool head, he could get by without too much trouble from the guards and could always find a way of making a few francs to buy tobacco. A skilled mechanic was valuable to the administration and cooks were highly sought after to work in the homes of the guards. Even the convict who swept the streets (there was an army of them) could get by with little trouble if he controlled himself.

Before 1920 there was no scheduled boat service to St. Laurent. The town, completely isolated from the rest of the world, existed for one purpose only. The distance from Cayenne (twenty hours by boat) limited the amount of contact the officials there had with St. Laurent. Because of the distance and discomfort of the voyage, governors were reluctant to make frequent inspection tours to St. Laurent and the penal administration had a free hand at running the territory.

For the guards and their families, the isolation could be wrenching; every day the same convict faces. The only contact with the outside was Albina, the Dutch village across the river. But Albina was even smaller than St. Laurent, and few of its townspeople spoke French, as few in St. Laurent spoke English or Dutch.

Iles Du Salut

Nine miles from the swampy coast of Kourou they appear as tiny islets jutting out of the ocean. From an approaching boat, they seem to be palm tree islands in the water. Whatever they resemble from offshore, no matter how pleasant they look, a prison term on the Iles du Salut amounted to no less than an excursion to hell.

Even on the mainland with its fevers and jungle, a man could still hope. The presence of free people in the Creole villages — no matter how poor — could give him some hope for the future. The possibility of escape gave him reason to dream.

On the islands there were no free men. There was no escape. Nothing on the islands could give a man the slightest hope. The sound of the surf pounding on the rocks and the bark of the guards was all that was heard on the islands and all that one could expect to hear.

Only the *true* outcasts among the convicts were sent to the islands. After 1873, Royale, the largest island (twenty-eight hectares), held the most dangerous convicts sent to Guiana; those thought most likely to escape, and those who had proved themselves unbreakable on the mainland. Also, men who had recently been liberated from solitary confinement on St. Joseph were kept on Royale.

At the turn of the century, when over seven hundred prisoners were held on Royale, the island was circled by a well-kept road that permitted access to all parts of the island. Crews of convicts were always weeding and clearing the bush that continuously tried to take over. Attempts were made to grow food and raise animals, but for the most part supplies to keep the island stocked came from the outside.

Supplies were often scarce. The hospital, which served convicts as well as guards, frequently ran short of equipment, and surgeons lacking an anesthetic resorted to ether or rum in order to operate. A shortage of syringes in 1920 made injections impossible, rendering the morphine supply useless. The next year when the syringes arrived, the morphine had disappeared.

One was less likely to contract malaria on the islands, but a good many men there shivered with fever from cases contracted on the mainland. The quinine supply was often limited and was given only to the most extreme cases.

The only contact with the outside world was the twice-monthly steamer from Cayenne which brought more prisoners and guards, as well as supplies. It was extremely difficult for a civilian not connected with the penal administration to gain entrance to the islands. An outsider could go to St. Laurent with few problems — probably raising the eyebrows of the police, but little more if he kept quiet. Cayenne was open to all, but the islands were cloaked in secrecy; visits were discouraged and rarely occurred.

While Royale was tortuous even at the best of times, St. Joseph (separated from Royale by several hundred feet) made Royale seem like a vacation colony, since it existed entirely for punishment.

Four hundred prisoners (150 in solitary confinement) were held on St. Joseph serving terms ranging from six months to five years. The island had no other function. There was no bustle of convicts as on Royale and silence reigned, since making noise in the cells was forbidden. The only sound came from the cells on the extreme end of the prison, for these held the insane — those who had cracked while serving their sentence.

Before the Kourou expedition, the three-island group was known by various names including "Devil's Islands." When Iles du Salut came into use in 1763, the name Devil's Island was applied to the smallest island on account of the dangerous currents that made landing on the island difficult. It was no more than a stone's throw from the other two, but isolated by the strong currents that separated it from Royale and St. Joseph.

Devil's Island couldn't be reached by boat every day, so a cable was constructed to link the island with Royale. Food and supplies were put in a basket and sent across when the sea was too rough.

Only half the size of Royale, it was a small leper colony before being used as a prison. Fewer than one hundred prisoners served time on Devil's Island during the one hundred years of the penal colony and no more than thirty were there at one time.

Only déportés (political offenders) were sent to Devil's Island after 1894. At times, no guard was stationed on the island. The prisoners were not made to work (since they were not sentenced to hard labor but to "imprisonment in a fortified enclosure") and their lives were the easiest in the prison colony. Food was sent regularly, and wine was part of the official ration. At least one governor of Guiana became enraged by prison officials who constantly communicated the complaints of déportés while ignoring those of transportés, saying, "They were sentenced to imprisonment, so treat them like prisoners."

But wine or no wine, Devil's Island was perhaps the most undesirable location in the prison colony. There were usually no more than a dozen prisoners on the island. They all lived in small huts apart from each other. They were dumped there and forgotten. It was like being marooned on another planet — all idea of the outside world disappeared. Every day, the same rocks and the same sharks offshore. A few kept small vegetable gardens near their huts, but most just paced the desolate shoreline and stared out to sea.

Nor would they acknowledge each other after a while. They had all recounted every detail of their lives to one another a thousand times and nothing could be gained by idle chatter.

As for escape from the Iles du Salut . . . one could only wish! A few did try — they attempted to put together rafts of bamboo and set off into the boiling water. It was extremely difficult to construct and hide anything on the islands on account of the ever-present guards. But there were a small number of successful escapes and the records allow that at least one man was able to make it to freedom.

Most of those who set out from the islands either drowned, were eaten by sharks or crashed back onto the islands where the rocks would tear them to pieces. Many times, escapees made it to the mainland, but were picked up immediately by alerted guards. There was no other direction to go, since a long sea voyage required a vessel much stronger than anything that could be obtained or built on the islands. Of course, there have been the boasters who claim to have escaped from the islands, Henri (Papillon) Charriére being the best known. But the few who actually did escape from the islands became the secret heroes of the prison colony.

In America, the name 'Devil's Island' became synonymous with the prison colony. In France it was 'Cayenne,' but like Devil's Island, Cayenne was one of the smaller units of the prison colony. Cayenne never rivaled St. Laurent in number of prisoners for there were never more than thirteen hundred there at any one time, and usually less than eight hundred.

Cayenne was without doubt the most desirable location for a prisoner to be sent. The convicts were kept five blocks from the center of town in three stone buildings. The camp was not walled, but enclosed by a simple iron fence. Most prisoners worked outside the camp and had the run of the town during the day. Some slept at the homes of their employers and some were entrusted with the education of their employers' children; others worked as butlers and cooks. All of the prisoners in Cayenne were able to make enough money to buy tobacco and rum. If a man was discreet, he could keep a Creole mistress and sleep with her several afternoons a week.

Technically, convicts in Cayenne were supposed to have the best behavior records in the prison colony, but like anything else in Guiana a transfer to Cayenne could be bought by all but the most depraved convicts. This is not to say that Cayenne was a paradise for all the convicts who lived there, but a man could get by if he watched his step. He wouldn't be subjected to the abuse and brutality that went on in the jungle camps or in St. Laurent during a brutal regime.

Officials had high hopes for article IV of the transportation act, authorizing women to be sent as prisoners to Guiana. The French government's goal of populating French Guiana couldn't be achieved with men alone and it was planned that male prisoners would, upon release, marry and have families in Guiana with Creole women.

There *were* Creole women in the colony, but not nearly enough for all the libérés. Marriages did occur between Creoles and ex-convicts and acceptance by local families of white libérés was quite good, with no stigma attached to the interracial couples. They were well received in Creole villages and even today, quite a few in French Guiana know that their grandfather or great uncle was a convict. Far from being ashamed of their lineage, it is considered downright chic in certain circles.

But very few of the libérés were eligible bachelors after their release. Even the poorest Creole women would sneer at the majority of libérés, most of whom became hopeless drunks upon release from prison. The local population had watched them being herded around like animals for too long.

During the first year of transportation, Governor Sarda-Garigas hoped to start populating French Guiana with marriages between convicts and prostitutes brought from Martinique. Released from custody and shipped to Ile Royale, the fifteen who arrived refused to marry any of the convicts there. Angered by their refusal, Sarda-Garigas sent them all to Montagne d'Argent.

They stayed in the heart of the jungle for several weeks, offering themselves to anyone who took their fancy or had some rum. They created havoc, provoking fights between the men. Such chaos ensued that the Catholic sisters (who had been sent to supervise them) demanded that they be sent elsewhere. The prostitutes were soon evacuated and returned to Martinique. The only "populating" that resulted from their stay was an epidemic of syphilis among the prisoners.

Governor Sarda-Garigas was forced to leave in disgrace after the episode, and his replacement Governor Baudin offered to permit convicts from France to bring their wives or else to have them sent to Guiana later on. But most convicts were not married and those who were, very often were divorced by their wives after conviction. French law made divorce relatively easy for the wives of convicted felons and very few followed their husbands to Guiana.

Meanwhile in French jails, only women who volunteered could be sent to Guiana. Those who agreed to come were prompted by desperation, as Guiana appeared to be an improvement over the stone cells in France. Only childless women between the ages of twenty-five and thirty-five could volunteer. They were promised that after six months of incarceration, they could marry and be given conditional freedom to live with their husbands. They were to be guarded and supervised by the Catholic sisters of St. Joseph of Cluny and separated at all times from the male prisoners.

Aboard the convict ship, it became clear to all what type of woman was going to colonize French Guiana. One of the ship's officers commented: "Insolent, unsubdued, quarrelsome, accusing, lying and deplorably immoral, they make the most patient guard lose his head. With their dreadful seductive powers they are most disgusting, knowing that on account of their sex, the discipline meted out to them is restricted. They are a much cruder bunch than the men."

Most of these woman had been convicted of infanticide, abortion and long-term prostitution. Certainly some of them had committed other crimes, mostly crimes of passion. Women who had lost their heads once, when finding a husband or lover in bed with another woman, were herded together with prostitutes who had been convicted thirty times. There was even a farmer's wife who had killed her two children and given the corpses to the pigs to eat.

At first, these women were kept in a special section of the camp at St. Laurent. Soon they were moved to new quarters in Mana kept by the Catholic sisters. Their courtship to libérés, strictly supervised, took place every Thursday morning. A limited number of men were permitted to visit, and the women made themselves up as best they could. They received their suitors in small booths that had been set up, always under the supervision of the nuns. Outside, a military guard stood watch and was called in at the first sign of trouble.

These women never had any trouble finding a willing man to marry. There were over seven hundred men for each potential wife. The first marriage in 1859 was an event of great pomp, very important to the plan to populate Guiana. All the important figures in the colony were present, from the governor on down. This is what Paris wanted to see; soon, they hoped, the children of these convict couples would populate the colony — their careers depended on it.

But it didn't work out that way. The first child born to convict parents (with the Director of the prison as godfather) died at an early age. Throughout the next few years this occurred with alarming regularity — over fifty percent of the children born to these convict couples died in infancy. And the number of sterile female convicts began to astound the prison doctor. Because of these disturbing reports Dr. Jean Orgeas, a specialist in female fertility, was sent to Guiana to investigate. From his investigation he concluded the following:

"From the beginning of 1859 to 1864, about four hundred couples have formed and live in the Maroni region. The proportion of childless marriages is enormous and the number of abortions — spontaneous and otherwise — is considerable. It appears that the white race has a very difficult time reproducing in this climate and the family environment of the new offspring is deplorable. From this, I conclude that this new race be halted."

Perhaps the good doctor was not aware of the conditions that made these women marry. Marriage meant release from prison and the suffocating grip of the nuns. Most of the women returned to prostitution, pimped by their new husbands. They were known to sleep with several men (for pay) on their wedding nights. The life that was prescribed — that of scratching away at the Guiana soil on one of the farms on the St. Jean road — was without doubt less attractive than setting up in a shack and selling their bodies in the Chinese quarter of St. Laurent.

Not all ended as whores. Those who refused to marry stayed with the Catholic sisters and were put to work sewing and tending the convent garden. Very few, if any, tried to escape and it was unlikely that any of the men escaping by canoe would consider taking women along. Escapees were well aware of the disputes that arose in the canoes and didn't want to bring women along to complicate matters even further.

Of the female prisoners brought to Guiana, the best remembered was one known as the 'Crazy Nun,' since she was often seen in the streets of St. Laurent babbling to herself and praising the name of God. It was thought that she was from a noble family that had lost its fortune. Well educated, she worked in France as headmistress in a private school until, in a jealous rage, she tried to poison her lover. Condemned to twenty years at hard labor, she was influenced by the nuns to confess her sins, and became determined to dedicate her life to Christ.

Not wanting to waste the talents of an educated woman (most of the female convicts were illiterate), the nuns arranged for her to teach at the local convent school. But as time went on, her religious fervor became too much for even the Catholic sisters. At the end of her sentence she continued to teach for awhile, until her insanity took over and she finished up walking the streets of St. Laurent with a Bible in her hand.

By the turn of the century, when it was finally decided to suspend the transport of female convicts, only thirteen remained among more than 5,000 male convicts. Not a single child of the convict marriages survived. Until the very last convoy in 1938, the French government never stopped proposing ways to populate Guiana with convict marriages. Dozens of plans were put forth — the last being one to integrate Arab prisoners with their families in 1930. An enlightened governor at the time rejected this with the question, "Why do we waste our time with this when we know quite well they'll all end up as prostitutes in the Chinese village?"

THE ONE WAY TICKET

French criminal courts sentenced nearly 70,000 men and women to equatorial banishment in French Guiana. Some were mass killers, others were bicycle thieves. A few — very few — were innocent, victims of judicial error or police frame-up. Whatever the crime and regardless of sentence, one fact remains: hardly any ever saw France again.

French courts were not known for consistency in punishment. An extremely violent man with several murders under his belt would arrive to serve ten years at hard labor (often less), while in the same convoy other murderers were condemned to hard labor for life. It was largely up to the sentencing judge.

Rural judges had the worst reputation. An offense for which a defendant in Paris served several months in prison could garner five years at hard labor in the outside provinces. During World War I it was most severe, and teenagers given the responsibility for farms and families — their fathers dead or in the army — got little sympathy from judges and were condemned to le bagne.

On the back of every French franc note, in a box toward the bottom, is Article 139 of the French penal code. It states that those who counterfeit or falsify currency can be sentenced to hard labor for life upon conviction. The bagne received a number of men convicted under this statute and almost always to the maximum penalty.

In cases of crimes of passion committed in jealousy, the French judges were often known to show some leniency. The right of a man to protect the honor of his home was understood. No such understanding was shown to counterfeiters who went into competition with the state for profit.

The road to Devil's Island began after a man was sentenced to his term of penal servitude, relegation or political deportation. Upon conviction the transporté lost his civil rights and from that moment on he was subject to the penal laws of the bagne. In France, after conviction, discipline was very strict. All prisoners were treated like those who had been sentenced to death.

Whether a man had been convicted in the courts of Paris, Toulon or Algiers, the preparation for his transport to Guiana was the same. In metropolitan France, from the central prisons near Paris or from provincial jails, the convoys were assembled by rail-cars which had been consigned exclusively for convict transport. From all parts of the country these rail-cars slowly made their way to La Rochelle. Upon arrival the prisoners were transferred offshore by ferry to the Ile de Ré.

From 1873, the concentration prison on the Ile de Ré held all the men awaiting shipment to Guiana. Often a backlog was created since the twice-yearly convoys were often late. Some convicts remained on the Ile de Ré for over a year. The discipline on the island never let up.

On the Ile de Ré, the only chance to hide money for later escape was by use of a plan, a small tube which unscrewed in the middle. Bank notes or jewels could be hidden inside. The tube had to be made from a non-corrosive material and the metal used varied, depending on the man's wealth. The richest convicts had theirs made from gold or ivory, while less affluent prisoners made do with aluminum. Once inserted in the anus and lodged in the intestine, only the most extensive finger search by the guards could reveal its presence — and this was something few guards wanted to do. Hope of escape and eventual freedom depended on the safe keeping of one's plan.

Everyone was on the lookout for wealthy criminals known to be "loaded." Curious eyes watched them every time they went to the latrine. One never knew when on of his "comrades" might pounce on him for the money. It became even more difficult if he came down with dysentery, a common ailment in the bagne.

In addition to money, a plan would sometimes contain a tool set with a small saw, strong enough to cut through handcuffs and a skeleton key to open the lock of a dungeon — all of great use during an escape.

The morning of embarkment fascinated all of France. Between five and seven hundred of France's worst criminals were marched from the stone fortress to the quay. Security was extremely tight, and soldiers pointed bayonets at the convoy while they walked through the streets of St. Martin, the village next to the prison. The soldiers were supplemented by police and guards from the penal administration. The convicts, dressed in coarse brown uniforms for the sea voyage with kit bags slung across their backs, shuffled rather than walked since their shoes were made of rough wood and chafed their feet.

Most of the bayonet-wielding soldiers were blacks from the colonial regiment of Senegal, specially recruited for the march. Mass insurrection was always feared, since these convicts had nothing to lose.

What they knew of French Guiana was only rumors, and it was rare that any of these prisoners had occasion to meet a convict who had already served time in the bagne. When an escaped convict from Guiana was apprehended in France, he was always segregated from the other prisoners on the Ile de Ré.

Most prisoners were not aware of the doublage, the regulation that would force most of them to reside in French Guiana for the rest of their lives. It was not mentioned during their trials, and many knew nothing about it until their arrival in French Guiana. For those sentenced to life at hard labor, the regulation didn't matter anyway. Two-thirds of the 4,000 transportés in Guiana in 1928 had been sentenced to over seven years, which meant perpetual exile in the colony. For the rest, condemned to less than seven years, many would become exiles as a result of extra years added to their sentence while in Guiana.

Emotions were mixed at St. Martin. The bagne had a reputation as a prison where escape was easy. Each time a man managed to escape, his name and story were flashed across the newspapers of France. Each year there were dozens of such reports, but no mention of the recaptures that took place weeks and months later, or of the skeletons found in the jungle or the shark-eaten corpses that washed ashore. In their ignorance, most were happy to leave France and the grim fortress on the Ile de Ré. The most naive of the prisoners were convinced that they would be in Rio de Janeiro before the end of the year with a drink in one hand and a girl in the other.

Most knew that they would probably never see either France or their families again. One-third of those transported after the turn of the century were married, and most of their wives would divorce them. Their children would forget them, the young ones would be told that their fathers were dead. The stigma of a husband, father or son in the bagne was nothing to advertise — they were a stain and an embarrassment to all concerned.

In fact, they were considered dead even before they left France. Along the narrow streets of St. Martin, from all over France, the curious arrived to watch the convoy leave for

French Guiana. Some were fascinated by the herd and wielded cameras to capture macabre souvenirs of men about to disappear. More touching were the relatives who came to see their loved ones off. From the assemblage of onlookers, a mother would catch a glimpse of her son being prodded by a bayonet-wielding black soldier and burst into tears — she knew that she would never see her son again since no one returned from the bagne.

During the march an aura of dread pervaded the streets. Generations of French children had been scolded with the warning, "If you keep up like that you'll end up in Cayenne." Only the guillotine was more frightening than banishment to French Guiana — and for most the hideous reputation would prove accurate.

The earliest transports of convicts to Guiana were made in sailing vessels provided by the French Navy. When the Navy was finally relieved of the task of transporting convicts to overseas penal settlements, a commission was set up to select a private company to do the job. In 1891, the Steamship Navigation Company of Nantes (La Compagnie Nantaise de Navigation à Vapeur) was chosen.

This company built vessels expressly for convict transport, or altered already existing ships to accommodate the convoys. As many as eight hundred convicts and two hundred officers, guards and sailors were transported in a large convoy to Guiana. Their first ship to make the voyage with a convict cargo was the *Ville de St. Nazaire.* It was succeeded by the *Caledonie* and then by the *Loire.*

During World War I, the convoys to Guiana were suspended and the *Loire* was put into use as a troop carrier. Torpedoed by the Germans in the Mediterranean, it stayed afloat until reaching the Greek islands where it was to be repaired. On entering a bay for dry-dock work, it swerved out of control and sank before reaching the dock.

After the war the Nantes company, still under contract to the Ministry of Colonies to provide convict transport, looked for a ship to replace the sunken *Loire*. It found a German ship, the *Douala* which was ceded to France in the armistice and approached the *Loire* in maritime specification.

Constructed in 1912 under the name *Armanistan*, this steamer was 100 meters long, 16 wide and weighed 3,500 tons. "Redecorated" for convict transport and re-christened the *Martinière*, it served all transports to Guiana until 1937, when it was sold to the General Transatlantic Company as the penal colony was under suppression. It was used for one more trip to Guiana in 1938, under a last-ditch effort to keep the penal colony alive.

During the months before the outbreak of World War II, the *Martinière*, scheduled for demolition, made several final voyages to the Caribbean. It was sunk during a German air raid in 1940.

The ship was specially constructed to provide transport to Guiana in the least time with the lowest possibility of convict riot. The voyage took between fifteen and twenty days depending on the weather — longer if the ship stopped in Algiers.

The contract of April 12th, 1921 between the French Ministry of Colonies and the Nantes company spelled out in detail the conditions under which the convicts would be transported to Guiana. The price-per-convict was set at 1000 francs, and cages were made of iron to isolate prisoners from the rest of the ship. Often the regulations set out in this contract were not respected. If the capacity of the ship's hold was exceeded, no further provisions could be made at the last moment.

It was not a pleasure cruise. The cages were 250 feet long and 8 feet wide and each was packed with ninety men. Only the strongest got to sleep in the available hammocks. For the weak and the old who couldn't fight, it was just too bad. They spent the entire voyage sleeping on the floor, which was filthy with vomit and excrement from latrine buckets that tipped over in rough seas.

The port-holes were opened only after the ship was out to sea. The men sat for the first several hours sweating and gasping for air.

As the engines started up and waves began to pound the ship, men who had never been to sea before got sick. The stench from all of them together, unwashed, vomiting and some with dysentery, was appalling.

The captain economized as much as he could on food and medicine for the convicts. The food was brought down below in large buckets. If the sea was rough and it spilled, the meal was lost. It would not be replaced, for this was a private ship run for profit.

The relégués had a separate cage and were not forced to shave their heads as the convicts were. If they wanted, they could keep moustaches and were permitted to supplement their ration. Technically at least, they had not been stripped of their civil rights.

More than anything, the guards feared an insurrection aboard the convict ship. All precautions had been taken against the possibility, and the cages were patrolled day and night by armed guards. Steam hoses were fitted inside the cage and could be turned on if trouble started, scalding the men inside and bringing order in seconds.

The worst punishment the ship could offer the unruly was a spell in the hot cells. These were located above the boilers, where little air could penetrate. The punished man was chained down with his hands behind his back. After a few hours even the most rebellious would scream to be let out and would make no more trouble for the rest of the voyage. The heat was too much to take. This type of treatment was not spelled out in the Nantes contract, as the text stated only that "isolation cells meet the requirements of naval discipline."

Normally several convicts died during the sea voyage to Guiana. When this happened, the body was wrapped in an old sail cloth and buried at sea. The engines were stopped while the "ceremony" took place and started up again when the corpse disappeared in the water.

For an hour every morning the prisoners were let out of their cages and brought on deck for exercise. Most would have preferred to stay below because of sea sickness. They paced under the watchful eyes of the guards, while the sailors hosed down the cages with sea water and other guards searched for knives or other contraband.

When the ship arrived in the tropics, the heat turned the cages into one big hot cell. Most of the prisoners spent the day huddled around the port holes to breath and look for signs of land. The heat became unbearable as the ship approached the equator. Their nerves began to wear thin from confinement and anticipation of what awaited them in Guiana. Relief finally came when land was sighted. Whatever awaited them in Guiana seemed preferable to the tortures of the convict ship.

The prison administration would be informed of the proximity of the ship several days in advance by cable. The entrance of the Maroni river was marked and patrolled that day, for it was tricky to navigate such a large vessel in the brown water. Sand bars could be hidden several feet below and convict-rowed pilot boats guided the Martiniere 25 miles upriver to St. Laurent.

From inside their cages, the convicts got their first look at the Guiana forest through the port holes. Bright green vegetation and enormous trees covered the river's bank like a solid wall. Brightly colored parrots flew close to the ship and just as quickly retreated to the jungle's safety. After the long voyage, they were impressed by the savage beauty of the river and its banks. The excitement became frenzied when canoes filled with bare-breasted natives paddled by the ship.

With St. Laurent in sight, a small tender approached the ship and picked up the highest officials. Dressed in immaculate white suits, they were met at the dock by other officials dressed exactly the same way. All of them retreated to the customs shed where sealed instructions and documents were turned over to the appropriate official.

The entire village of St. Laurent assembled near the waterfront to watch the arrival from France. It was the town's great (and only) occasion and it took place just twice a year.

In the front ranks of the crowd stood the highest officials of the penal administration, surrounded by their families. Next to the Director were his assistants and representatives from Cayenne — only rarely was the governor there personally. Behind the high officials stood the guards and police of St. Laurent. All would have much work to do, since the ship's arrival heralded the town's busy season.

The rest of the town's populace was scattered to all sides of the official assemblage: wives and children of guards dressed in summer dresses and shorts; Creoles in multicolored cotton frocks, laughing and showing their white teeth, often capped in gold; and bush-negroes from upriver in loin-cloths, the women wearing brassieres to cover their breasts for the occasion. Even the Chinese left their shops to watch.

In back of everyone else were the libérés. Frighteningly emaciated and dressed in rags, they looked on with little expression, leaning against their wheelbarrows and spitting into the dust. The newly arrived convicts were a forbidding flash into their own pasts.

When the ship finally made its way next to the pier and its engines stopped, the prison doctor went aboard accompanied by several guards. He checked for signs of epidemic among the prisoners and had the sickest men taken ashore. His work finished, he withdrew onto the pier and the head guard took over.

From the bowels of the ship, men who had been at sea for weeks made their way single file onto the dock. They looked around as though they were on another planet. For those from the large cities of France the equatorial forest was striking. Those born and raised on farms looked with awe at the negroes — most had never seen a black before. Though nearly ninety degrees, the hot air felt good to breath after weeks in the hold.

With the entire town looking on, all 700 were led from the dock to the gates of the *Camp de la Transportation.*

Still dressed in the heavy woolens they had worn from France, the heat made them perspire profusely. Soon other convicts arrived with thin white and red striped suits.

Inside the gate the roll was called. All responded save the men who had died or those who had been put immediately in the hospital. This formality taken care of, the lot of convicts assembled for the traditional "welcoming speech" by the director of the penal administration. It usually went like this:

"You have arrived here to pay for crimes committed against France. You are all criminals and do not deserve the least bit of mercy. For those who behave themselves, life will not be made unbearable. For those who cause trouble, we have excellent methods of punishment at our disposal. I know that most of you have ideas of escape — forget them! You will be given a great deal of freedom in the camps and in town. Don't ever forget that the real guards here are the jungle and the sea."

When the speech was over, the whole convoy was locked up until the next day. Sometimes the guards let an old convict enter the cells to instruct the new arrivals on life in the colony. At dusk, a small oil lamp was lit in the center of the barracks and the mosquitos began to attack. The men began to slap at them; the slapping would go on for the rest of their lives.

Some would stay in St. Laurent for several weeks awaiting assignment to one of the jungle camps. The relégués were transferred to St. Jean the next day. The most dangerous men were isolated immediately for shipment to Ile Royale.

THE GOOD, THE BAD AND THE SAVAGE

What type of men were sent to the bagne? Like anywhere else, there were good ones and bad ones. This went for the prisoners as well as the guards. Without doubt, some of the convicts were extremely violent killers and some of the guards were out and out sadists but these were exceptions.

The crime that sent to a man to French Guiana had little to do with his actions once he arrived. Murderers sometimes became model prisoners while pickpockets sometimes became killers. A few of the guards risked their lives to save certain prisoners and others shot prisoners in cold blood.

Dr. Louis Rousseau, chief medical officer of the Guiana prisons in the early 1920s, remarked that among the convict nurses, "one could find men who cared for the sick with greater compassion and enthusiasm than could be found in any other hospital in the world." These convict nurses made no distinction between prisoner and guard in the treatment of the sick. They were even known to steal supplies, or pay out of their own pockets for medicine and treatments that were not normally available. Some became so skilled in the treatment of tropical diseases that they could cure patients that the doctors had given up for dead.

Other convict nurses had no such inclination or ability, but sold drugs and foodstuffs intended for the sick in order to buy tobacco and rum.

Many accounts of the French Guiana penal colony recall the guards as a sadistic and brutal lot, passing a dull afternoon by flogging disfavored convicts and shooting those who protested. A few lived up to this reputation, but they were exceptions, and even their fellow guards avoided them.

In fact, contact between convicts and guards was not always hostile. So far away from France in the isolation of French Guiana, they became dependant on each other. The convicts needed the guards to better their condition and the guards needed the convicts to line their pockets.

In many respects the guards were prisoners, much like the convicts. They didn't have to hack away in the jungle cutting down trees and they were not forced to be there — still, they were just as likely to contract malaria. They arrived in Guiana under contract for two year stints before returning to France on paid leave. For most, French Guiana was no paradise, it was a job and perhaps the only one they were capable of holding.

Most of the guards came from poverty-stricken backgrounds, and their official position in the bagne represented their only real chance to advance into the "respectable" world.

Not that they were proud of their profession. When people back in France asked what they did for a living, most replied in a vague manner that they worked for the colonial service. It was a vile insult among members of the French underworld to call someone a *guarde chiourme* (galley slave overseer). This is how they were referred to by convicts all over France and by some civilians too.

Over half of the guards were Corsicans who had fled the barren fields and slums of that island in search of steady work. The others came from all walks of life — some had already been prison guards in the hardest African military penitentiaries or the French Foreign Legion. A few were blacks from French Guiana itself, or the French West Indies. The blacks enjoyed the best reputation among the prisoners, as fair and never sadistic guardians who would never take part in the savagery that sometimes amused their white colleagues.

In asking what motivated a man to leave France and go to French Guiana to guard over men condemned to hard labor, it is important to recall working conditions in France during the time of the bagne. Twelve-hour days and six-day weeks were the norm in factories, longer on the farm. Colonial service appeared to be a way to escape this drudgery. Roger Flotat, who was a guard in Guiana described what inspired him to apply:

"I was twenty-eight years old, and worked at the Renault plant in Billancourt, near Paris. I lived in the sixteenth arrondissement in a small apartment on the fourth floor. When I looked out the window, I saw a man in a neighbor's courtyard, stretched out on a long chair. For some reason this man intrigued me and I wondered what he did for a living.

"When I mentioned him to my father, he told me that this man was a colonial officer on leave. He knew the family across the street and could introduce me to this man if I wanted.

"A few days later, I met this man over drinks. His name was Sauvée, chief of staff of the colonial penitentiary service on a six month leave. He said that he was recruiting guards for Guiana. I decided right then and there to apply."

After two medical exams, Flotat was selected and sailed to St. Laurent. Two days after arrival, he assumed his post. The only training given to him was a little advice over drinks from the older guards, "Watch out for the convicts, for they like to take advantage of a new guard."

Mireille Maroger, a lawyer, was one visitor to the penal colony whom the guards would never forget. After her visit she published a book that inspired the Guiana guards to bring legal action against her for libel and slander. She gives the following account of an interview with a Guiana guard on the ship to Cayenne: "When I asked him how a plan was extracted from a convict, he graphically explained his method. 'Laxatives are a joke, and besides the doctor doesn't approve. What we do is raise the man's arms and give him a good kick in the gut. Sometimes it sends the guy to the hospital.'"

Since it was officially against regulations for a convict under sentence to receive money from France, a guard would act as intermediary. The money was addressed to the guard and he would keep twenty-five percent for himself, handing the rest over to the prisoner. Usually the guards were honest, rarely keeping the entire sum. If it became known that a certain guard had cheated a convict, none of the other men would have their money sent through this guard again and he would stand to lose a great deal.

Bribery and theft were rampant in all the convict camps. Cooks regularly stole one-third of the food allotment intended for the prisoners and sold it on the convict black market. The same was true of the clothing supply and anything else that was distributed. Usually the guards looked the other way as long as they received their percentage.

Henri Bauve found the guards a very mixed lot. "One of them brought me home to dinner and treated me like family." Henri Bauve also remembered an incident that took place in St. Laurent with a completely different type of guard. "After unloading one of the supply boats, a man was covered with flour and asked one of the guards if he could go down to the river to wash. The guard refused this convict's request saying that it would soon be sundown. He ignored this guard and hurried off to the Maroni with a towel in his hands. The guard screamed, 'Bastard, I'll teach you to obey my orders!' and fired one shot from his revolver, hitting the man between his shoulders. He died the next day and nothing, of course, happened to the guard."

This case, however, *did* cause a stir. Though the guard wasn't prosecuted for murder, official reports indicate condemnation on the part of the prison administration. The guard in question was disciplined, as the penal administration considered cold-blooded murder of a prisoner to be serious business.

More sordid than the guards were their wives. Quite a few were said to have been prostitutes in France and, surrounded by hundreds of young men, they teased the convicts to no end, infuriating their husbands.

It was not uncommon for one of these women to take a young convict as a lover. Often, one selected a convict "maid" to work in her home for this purpose. While her husband was on duty, she could enjoy the company of the houseboy at will. It was a precarious situation for all involved. If the husband surprised them in bed, it usually meant a bullet in the head of the convict, and the entire incident would be dismissed as attempted rape.

Still, it was worth the risk for many of the young convicts. That situation would bring about many favors and a soft life, away from the jungle camps and fever. Some of the husbands tolerated and even participated in these affairs, and love affairs involving the guard, his wife and the houseboy were not unheard of. After all, Guiana held few other distractions.

Homosexuality among the prisoners was very common. The majority had been heterosexual before being sent to Guiana, but many of the younger and weaker convicts were forced into homosexuality by the older, stronger men. Older convicts who initiated homosexual liasons with younger prisoners were known as fort-à-bras (strong arms) and they were just that, for most had served years in the bagne or in African military prisons and knew all there was to know about convict vice.

Sometimes they began to pressure the younger ones into becoming their môme as far back as Ile de Ré, but this was difficult as the strict discipline inhibited contact. On the convict ship, however, offers of tobacco and protection turned to threats and beatings. Few were able to resist and by the time they arrived in St. Laurent, all the fort-à-bras had their mômes. In Guiana, those who rebelled were beaten into submission or fought over by the other convicts. Most mômes tolerated their status, since their fort-à-bras could make life easier and protect them.

According to Dr. Rousseau, "Of these homosexual practices indulged in by about sixty percent of the convicts, not only have the prison authorities done nothing to prevent it, but very often have profited from it." Known homosexual couples were intentionally separated (the môme sent to a different camp) and not reunited until the right guard had been paid off. The guards all knew who was "married" to whom, and the fort-à-bras always had cash on hand to pay the bribe.

The relégués were more openly deviant than the convicts under sentence. They were of an entirely different character than the transportès, and are still hated by the last surviving ex-prisoners in French Guiana.

The relégation was not a prison sentence, but rather a banishment. To become a relégue, a man needed to be convicted of at least four small crimes — theft, vagrancy, and bad checks to name a few. After serving his last sentence in a French jail, he was put on the convict ship and sent to Guiana. Many judges, however, were reluctant to send someone to the bagne for four small offences, so relégués didn't get sent to French Guiana until their twentieth conviction. A relégué did not lose his civil rights, and was technically a free man within the confines of the colony. When they were first sent to Guiana in 1885, it was hoped that they would start small farms in the interior and help build up the colony.

The relégués showed no such inclination. After several years of letting them wander the streets, a camp fifteen miles from St. Laurent was set up. Despite their technical freedom within the colony, they were soon subjected to conditions similar to, and in many respects worse than those in the convict camps. They were not obliged to wear the red and white uniforms of the convicts but were issued them, since they had to be clothed. They were fed the same rations as at St. Laurent and, since they were unruly, guards of the penal administration were sent to watch over them. Legally they had no sentence to serve but in effect they had life sentences. They could be put in solitary confinement and were more likely to be abused by the guards than transportés in the convict camps.

Isolated from the civilian towns, St. Jean was a nest of vice. Several of the relégués were active transvestites and at one time, a ballet composed entirely of these men performed for the camp at large. St. Jean's fort-à-bras went to great lengths to supply their mômes with what they wanted.

The contraband at St. Jean included women's underwear and silk stockings. Guards at St. Jean were amused by all this and more than eager to look the other way, provided they received their payoff.

These conditions, when made known to the transportés at St. Laurent, filled them with disgust — a disgust still alive today. The convict camps were by no means a seminary, but even in the cesspool of the bagne there were limits, and to the transportés, the relégués went beyond these limits. For them, the relégué was a degenerate — too lazy to work and lacking the courage to pull off a big job. Many transportés had been condemned for one crime, committed in a jealous rage over a woman, and the relégué transvestite seemed to them the lowest a man could sink to.

When an unfortunate môme contracted syphilis, he was sent to rot at the relégué camp for incurables. In the bagne, eighteen-year old convicts found themselves in the company of hardened men from Biribi, the roughest of the African military prisons. The young ones would die first, since first offenders and mass murderers were herded together in the bagne.

Feared and hated more than any guard were the executioners. Drawn from the convict ranks, they publicly guillotined any man condemned to death in the penal colony. It was a sought-after post, despite the threats it incurred from other convicts. British novelist W. Somerset Maugham visited St. Laurent in the 1930's and based his short story *An Official Position* on a convict executioner murdered by fellow prisoners.

When there was a vacancy, the chief guard asked for volunteers from the prisoners assembled at roll call. All of them muttered obscenities under their breath; no one would come forward. But the next day, many discrete letters found their way into the guard's mail box from convicts who offered their "services." After a few weeks the chosen man moved quietly out of the barracks into the executioners hut and waited for work.

The guillotine was stored in a small shed near the Maroni river and was locked up in storage until it was needed. Nicknamed 'The Gay Widow,' the first one used in French Guiana was locally made, but after several very messy executions (the blade was badly weighted and not sharp enough) a new one arrived from France. A second guillotine was stored in another shed and was used at St. Jean. There was another guillotine on Ile Royale, but it was rarely used. There were no executions in Cayenne.

Hespel, nicknamed 'The Jackal,' was the best known of the executioners. During his tenure he beheaded more than thirty convicts. He holds the distinction of being the only executioner to die under the knife of his own guillotine. After his liberation, no longer housed and clothed by the penal administration and unable to find employment because of his past status as executioner, he headed into the jungle. From a small shack in the forest, he tracked down escaping convicts and ripped them open for their plans. Finally one of the wounded men escaped and denounced Hespel. Brought to St. Laurent, Hespel was tried and condemned to death.

He was executed by Leon La Durrelle, his former assistant and successor. La Durrelle came to Guiana in 1924 after killing his mistress. After executing over twenty men, he was pardoned of the rest of his sentence and his doublage. When he returned to France in 1937, he was interviewed by *Paris-Soir*. "There are plenty of advantages in being an executioner in the bagne," he explained. "Most important is the comparative freedom. You can't imagine what freedom means in a place like that. All the fifteen years I was there, I received threats and my life was not safe, but I was more a free man than any of the others."

In 1938, only a year after he returned from Guiana, La Durrelle's new freedom came to an abrupt halt when he was found lying dead in a Paris street, stabbed in his back. Was this the revenge of an escaped convict? The code of vengeance against an old executioner is strong and his past is never forgotten. The crime was never solved.

A man could be sentenced to death for a variety of crimes while a convict in the bagne. The most serious was the murder of a civilian — rare, but it did occur. Then there was the murder of a guard or members of his family, also rare. Killing a fellow convict rarely resulted in the death penalty. These murders happened mainly at night in the barracks — the assailant would creep silently under the hammock of his victim and stab through the cloth. The alarm was not usually sounded until the next morning when the guard on duty discovered the corpse and the official inquiry began.

There were few, if any, witnesses. No convict would stand forward and accuse another in front of the guards — even if the accused was this man's worst enemy. To do so would bring down the enmity of the others in the barracks. If this man was to die, it could be arranged at some other time when it was convenient.

Many convicts were sent to the bagne after being sentenced to death in France and then pardoned by the President of the Republic. The sentence of hard labor for life in French Guiana was considered the worse punishment by many.

Eugene Boyer owed his life to Paul Gorgoloff. The two men didn't know each other and had never even heard of one another when Boyer was scheduled to die by the guillotine on May 7th, 1932. On May 6th, Gorgoloff assassinated French President Paul Doumer and the country was thrown into crisis. Boyer's lawyer immediately filed a last minute appeal, claiming that without a head of state, an execution could not take place. His execution was stayed and when the National Assembly chose Albert Lebrun as acting head of state on May 10th, he quickly commuted Boyer's sentenced to hard labor for life, not wishing to start his administration with an execution.

Boyer, a man with twenty-four hours to live before his reprieve, sailed to Guiana several months later and was held on Ile St. Joseph for seven years. Transferred to St. Laurent at the outbreak of World War II, he was employed as an accountant and made three unsuccessful escape bids. By 1950, with the bagne being liquidated, he fought all attempts to be returned to France. His position in Guiana as a convict employee of a mining company was much better than anything he could hope for in a French jail. In 1953, he sailed back to France and was interned in the grim Fontervault penitentiary. Finally paroled in 1957, he remade his life and was known as a model employee.

Before 1890, any man condemned to die by the Guiana *Tribunal Maritime Special* (T.M.S.) could appeal the verdict to the President of France. This, however, kept men on death row for many months, since communication between France and Guiana depended on the monthly freighter and the appeals process could take even longer. Power to pardon was turned over to the governor of the colony until 1925, when it again reverted back to the French President.

Death row was located in a special quarter of the St. Laurent prison and was constantly guarded by keepers specially recruited for the service. The cells measured five by seven feet, and the condemned man was chained to his bare wooden plank. They were the only convicts to be chained after 1924 and they were never let out.

When all avenues of appeal had been exhausted by the condemned man and the death warrant arrived on the desk of the Director, events moved rapidly. Most executions took place in St. Laurent, but a few were held on Ile Royale. The guillotine was removed from its shed, set up and tested with banana stems to see if the knife functioned properly. It was then moved to the interior courtyard where executions took place, and the executioner was often seen there the night before making last minute adjustments.

The eve of an execution was a night of great tension for the whole town of St. Laurent. None of the convicts slept and the guards didn't silence the barracks that night. None would dare enter the convict's cells. The streets of St. Laurent were deserted, since none of the guards were inclined to party and the bars and bordellos were closed.

Alone in his cell, the condemned man ate his last meal and was given a few shots of tafia and all the cigarettes he wanted. If he was illiterate, his last letter to his family was written by a priest.

At the crack of dawn six armed guards entered the cell, removed the convict's chains and watched him as he ate his last breakfast — usually some more rum and cigarettes. The priest was present to give those who wished them the last rights.

In the barracks, thirty convicts were selected to witness and were lined up by the guillotine, fifteen on each side. When the condemned man entered the courtyard, all of them knelt down as if in prayer.

The guillotine, in use since before the French Revolution, may have been the most painless method of execution but it was by no means the cleanest. It rarely made a neat slice, but more likely an orgy of blood and brain tissue.

When the condemned man was brought up to the guillotine and his head placed in the yoke, all the kneeling convicts lowered their heads as the knife fell and decapitated its victim. An old convict, interviewed by William Willis, recalled a particularly gruesome execution. "When his head was cut off, the straps that held him broke under his struggles. There was so much life and fierceness in him that the headless chained body with blood gushing out of it started to jump around the guillotine. They say that the guards started to run, afraid that he would attack them. But the most terrible sight was the executioner; I'll never forget it. He was bathed in the man's blood from head to toe — there was not an inch of him that wasn't covered. He was really drenched."

When a convict committed a small offense the infraction was recorded in a guard's notebook. Twice a month, all those who had committed infractions were brought before the disciplinary commission. The usual punishment for fighting, lateness and refusal to work was several days in solitary confinement. More serious crimes such as escape or assault on a guard were tried by the Tribunal Maritime Special which met twice a year. Before trial, those detained were held in a special section of St. Laurent called the blockhaus. René Belbenôit spent months there while in detention for an attempted escape.

"Life in the blockhaus, I was to discover, never changes from year to year. Many of the prisoners will be dead when the day of their trial arrives, after weeks of waiting and suffering, of longing to get out. In detention for months, they show the wear of close confinement. There were some who were veritable skeletons; continued existence in a place where there is so little light and where they have to lie around breathing a tainted air which is hot and saturated with humidity soon makes them anemic. Their digestive systems do not function properly, they lose all desire to eat. They suffer from hookworm, from malaria — they need medical attention and exercise.

"By day they pace up and down and fret; for these are men who have rebelled at conditions, who had the courage and the will power to face the danger of escape rather than see themselves in the cesspool which is the prison colony. Any other civilized nation would have given them a chance to remake their lives, instead of sending them to death. Some of them committed a first felony in an excess of folly, caught in the cycle of circumstances as so often happens in life and are in no sense criminals. They are men who have energy, moral fiber and self respect who lost in the gamble for liberty with odds all against them, and they are now locked up like animals in close quarters with assassins, thieves and perverts. They are all men of action and confinement goes hard with their temperament."

The T.M.S. was comprised of a President, usually an army officer from Cayenne and two associates — one from the civil court and another from the penal administration.

The crimes dealt with here warranted the intervention of a defense counsel for the accused convict. The defense was carried out by a guard assigned to the defendant and most were conscientious, occasionally bringing about acquittals. Unlucky was the man accused of murder whose "lawyer" was not inclined to put up a serious defense, but merely asked the T.M.S. to have "indulgence."

Extra years at hard labor was the punishment usually meted out to men originally condemned to years of hard labor. For convicts under life sentence, it was long periods of solitary confinement. And there was the guillotine for murder or assault against a guard or civilian. The maximum sentence was five years in solitary confinement and the gap between that and the death penalty was even greater, since a man in the cells could be released after eighteen months.

The T.M.S. also had the power to classify a convict as "incorrigible" which meant a transfer to Royale or one of the hardest jungle camps.

The sentence of solitary confinement was carried out in the réclusion cells on St. Joseph. Absolute silence was demanded and many went insane from the loneliness and solitude. It wasn't until 1926 that convicts were given an hour of exercise per day.

The small cells had little ventilation. There was no ceiling, but iron bars where the guards who walked on a catwalk from up above could see all that went on below. In the morning coffee was brought, and then nothing until afternoon. The wooden plank that served as a bed in these cells was raised in the morning. This meant that men inside the cells had to either stand all day long or lie on the floor. For decades this measure had attracted criticism. Finally, after an appeal by the chief prosecutor of in Guiana in 1935, the Director of the penal administration ordered the following: "As a remedy, since the present condition promotes possible problems, please install a small stool in each cell."

Despite other fabrications in the book and film Papillon, Charriere did serve time in solitary confinement on St. Joseph. Next to the guillotine, St. Joseph was the harshest penalty imposed by the T.M.S. in Guiana. However, it can be argued that Guiana's jungle camps were worse.

FEVER ON THE EQUATOR

A five-minute walk in the jungle will dispel any romantic notions about the place. Every step requires a chop with a machete. Every yard is agony because of mosquitos which swarm and bite through the thickest clothing. Every hour lost is a nightmare. Only the well-supplied can spend more than a few weeks there.

There is little cause to fear French Guiana's anacondas, crocodiles and jaguars. The big animals that roam the forest will avoid you. They generally disappear without trace or sound when you are ten feet away. They won't attack unless you are careless and step on one while it sleeps.

The big killers in the jungle didn't need size. Before the arrival of Europeans, the Indians didn't seem to suffer much from malaria. The explorers brought measles and syphilis with them, and the negro slaves donated leprosy from Africa.

European convicts showed no resistance at all to the malaria present in French Guiana. It was only partially responsive to quinine, which was often in short supply anyway. Almost all the convicts and guards suffered from the disease to some degree. It was especially bad in the jungle camps, where prisoners worked knee-deep in the swamps with no protection from the mosquitos.

Dr. Louis Rousseau, who served as medical officer for the penal colony in the 1920s, reported that between 1901 and 1919, malaria caused 53,600 hospitalizations among prisoners and 1,345 deaths. A man with malaria would find his way to the hospital and stay there for a few days until his fever went down. Back in the swamps a week later, another attack would be forthcoming. Quite a few convicts spent a dozen periods in the hospital during a single year.

Another more deadly disease running rampant in the penal colony was ankylostomiasis. It was caused by a small parasite that entered the body by drilling a small hole through the skin, usually on the feet. French Guiana's convicts were ideal victims since most of them were badly dressed and fed and walked on the jungle paths barefoot.

Once inside the body, the parasites travelled through the tissues and into the small intestine where they matured. In the worst cases, the parasites began living off the blood of its victim causing anemia and skin lesions. In some of the jungle camps, men in the last stages of the disease could be seen, more dead than alive. They were on the verge of starvation and looked mummified — almost walking zombies. When they collapsed, they were brought to the hospital to die. Their autopsy would show an enormously bloated liver and completely degenerated pancreas. Some would have survived if they had more to eat and shoes to wear, but this would have cut into the profits of the officials and other higher-ups.

Dr. Rousseau described the general sanitary conditions in the penal colony as an act of "moral bankruptcy as perpetuated by the prison administration." He concluded that "the convict ration which represents 2,475 calories daily is insufficient for hard labor under the torrid Guiana climate." And this was the officially claimed ration; the convict actually got considerably less, as a result of theft.

Very few men in the jungle camps could afford to buy extra food. Outside Cayenne and St. Laurent there was little chance to make extra money.

In the hastily built camps little attention was given to sanitation. Few could escape chronic dysentery from bad food and water. Few could escape tropical infection and jungle rashes.

But the convict feared leprosy more than any other disease. A few committed suicide when it was diagnosed rather than live out their last days rotting from its effects. It was a heartbreaking disease — all the more so since it normally struck toward the end of a man's sentence. It rarely hit a man who had been in French Guiana for less than five years, and a libéré with the disease was not permitted to go back to France even after his doublage was completed.

It started with swelling and loss of sensation in some part of the body. The doctor jabbed pins into the area; if the man didn't react, a further analysis was made by nasal scraping. If positive, the man was evacuated immediately to St. Louis Island in the middle of the Maroni, halfway between St. Laurent and St. Jean.

According to Dr. Hervé Floch, Director of the Pasteur Institute in French Guiana from 1938 to 1962, six percent of convicts sent to Guiana eventually contracted leprosy in one form or another. For Floch and other specialists in French Guiana during the bagne, leprosy was difficult to understand. No cases were diagnosed during the first thirty years of penal colony and most later statistics were widely disputed. Floch observed, however, that while convicts of all nationalities (Arabs, Europeans, Asians) seemed to contract the disease in equal numbers, European prisoners almost invariably contracted the more virulent lepromatous form, while Arabs contracted tuberculoid leprosy, which was milder.

Cases were seen regularly after 1883. When a report by a Dr. Thézé in 1916 stated that "leprosy hasn't greatly invaded the prisons" he was correct, in that few of the new cases involved convicts under sentence. Most of the victims were released libérés. St. Louis, opened in 1895 for convicts under sentence, had a population of twenty-one in 1897 and exceeded one hundred at certain times.

On St. Louis, the lepers lived out their final days in squalor. There were no guards on the island, and the doctors from St. Laurent came infrequently. There was not much they could do, as they had little time and few supplies. Chaulmoogra oil, the only drug in use at the time to arrest the spread of the disease, was in short supply — and it was not certain whether it worked at all. There was no cure. In time, a victim's hands would turn into claws and his face would be eaten away by the disease.

Once a day, a small canoe from St. Laurent arrived with food. It was left on the beach uncooked for the lepers to prepare, the canoeist hastily returning to St. Laurent. Nobody wanted to linger near the island.

The lepers had a canoe submerged in the river and at night they raised it to go to St. Laurent or Albina. They brought tafia from the Chinese with money they made raising chickens on the island. Once in a while a leper was found dead drunk in a gutter of St. Laurent. He had little to fear from the police, regardless of what he had done. All that they would do was escort him back to St. Laurent. He couldn't be arrested or tried — nor could he be convicted. Colin Rickards, a chronicler of the penal colony, put it this way: "Punishment meant men touching him and things touching him. It meant cells... and lepers were not wanted in the cells."

Nor could a leper escape. A healthy man might find refuge and sympathy among natives in neighboring countries, but a man in the final stages of leprosy could expect no help at all. He would be shunned, avoided and reported to the police at first sighting.

Escaping convicts from St. Laurent, however, sometimes took refuge on the island. They needed a place to buy supplies — a place where no one would look or want to look. The lepers were known to be more than willing to sell what was needed. It is also known that convicts on occasion bought leprosy-positive bacteria so that they could be transferred to St. Louis, in order to escape.

When a leper reached the end of his prison sentence, he was simply transferred to the civilian leper colony at Acarouany.

The three prison hospitals at St. Laurent, on Ile Royale and at Cayenne were always filled to capacity. Not only did these facilities lack space, but they were chronically short of supplies. Treatment of recognized diseases was impossible since the pharmacy didn't have the required drugs or a competent man to make up the prescriptions. Often enough, the doctors couldn't even make a diagnosis since they lacked proper equipment, or because the disease was unknown to them.

The doctors were French Army surgeons, detailed for two-year tours of duty in the penal colony. They did the best they could under the conditions and with the materials they had at hand. They were over-worked and had to deal with dying men, corrupt officials and convicts who stole supplies. It has often been written that the doctors sent from France to serve in the Guiana prisons were the dregs of the medical profession. Perhaps the opposite was true, as the names of France's finest tropical medicine specialists figure in administrative records of the bagne. The civilian population of Guiana — though technically without access to the prison hospital — would go out of their way to be treated by the prison doctor if a complicated case arose.

At any one time, one-fifth of the convict population was sick in the hospital. A few months in one of the jungle camps would be enough to break the strongest individual. The penal colony had been created so that convicts would open up the interior, yet each project started would send the death rate soaring. Each convoy from France replaced the dead of the previous shipment. Each year over 1,000 new convicts arrived, but the convict population remained stable. As these statistics reached the desk of the Paris official responsible for the penal colony, new plans would be drawn up and the whole vicious cycle would start again.

In the hospital, as soon as the convict nurses realized that a man was dying, they made certain that any medicine made its way to others who might at least survive. As the dying man breathed his last, the convict mortician arrived with a stretcher and carried the still-warm corpse to the morgue. This was a lucrative job, as he could always search the corpse for gold teeth and a plan in the intestines. Most of the convicts were flat broke, or had given all their money to someone else for safe keeping. It made no difference for all the convicts got the same burial.

At St. Laurent, a flimsy wooden coffin was nailed together from discarded lumber. It was carried to the outskirts of town, where a large stand of bamboo separated the convict's burial ground from the civilian's. If the dead man had friends, they would plant a wooden cross into the ground and scratch his name on it. In time, the wood would rot and the grave — indistinguishable from all the others — would disappear in the weeds.

On the islands where space was at a premium, the dead man was wrapped in a old sheet with a heavy stone attached to it. The corpse was rowed to the middle of the Royale-St. Joseph channel and slipped into the sea. More often than not, before the package could sink, the sharks — ever-abundant near the islands — ripped it open and devoured the contents in an orgy of red blood and blue water. There were few tears from the convicts at these funerals — only fear, fear that the shark's next meal might be their own flesh.

Isolated from the easier prison centers at Cayenne and St. Laurent, life in the jungle camps went from bad to worse. The camps that dotted the road between Mana and St. Laurent were small stretches of bush burned, cleared and put into use by convict labor. The sleeping quarters were rough wood barracks that kept the rain out, but little else.

When a prisoner arrived in Guiana, he was placed in one of three categories: fit for road work, fit for jungle work or fit for light work. To be classified for light work meant that he was incapacitated — usually too old to work or lacking a limb. The great majority fit into the second category and were sent into the bush to chop trees or plant vegetables.

A typical day started at 5:30 am. In the dark, the men instinctively examined their ankles to see if a vampire bat had struck during the night. These bats had a painless bite, but injected an anticoagulant which caused loss of blood and the filthy incision infected easily.

By six, bread and a half pint of unsweetened coffee were given out. Tools were distributed and the entire camp headed out to the edge of the forest. If the assigned task was tree cutting, the daily quota was normally one cubic meter per man. The logs had to be stacked in the middle of the clearing, hundreds of yards from the tree line.

Most convicts worked without shoes, since those supplied were useless in the jungle. As the morning wore on, the heat became unbearable. Sweat poured freely and the mosquitos started their attack. Cutting a cubic meter of wood is not a difficult task for a man in good health, but most of the convicts suffered from malaria and dysentery. They staggered through the jungle, weak from fever and lack of proper food.

If a man failed to meet the quota, he was shut into one of the punishment cells that night on reduced ration. The next morning he arose to chop another meter of wood, weak from missing the previous evening's meal.

A brutal guard in charge of one of the camps could turn life into a non-stop hell. Under a more lenient official, conditions might improve, but not by much since the mosquitos continued to bite and the jungle continued to kill.

Convicts classified as "incorrigible" were sent to the tougher jungle camps. Charvein, situated seventeen kilometers from St. Laurent, was the worst. To lessen the possibility of them escaping, prisoners worked naked in the forest all day. Devoured by insects and cut by sharp vegetation, the most desperate resorted to self-mutilation to get transferred to the hospital in St. Laurent. Other methods used by certain convicts to get out of Charvein and into the hospital were horrifying. They breathed sulfur fumes to fake T.B. or rubbed castor bean into their skin to cause swelling.

The most brutal guards were sent to watch over the naked prisoners. They were bored and spent their time drinking tafia. They couldn't bring their wives because of the naked prisoners, so they were stuck in the middle of the bush without distraction.

Charvein was closed as a punishment camp in 1926. It continued to operate as a regular jungle camp after that, but incorrigible convicts were sent to Ile Royale or another camp several miles from Charvein called Godebert.

Along the Mana road in the afternoon, prisoners who had finished their quota for the day were free to collect butterflies. These were sold to the guards, who in turn sold them to collectors in Cayenne. It was the only way to make money for an escape or for extra rations.

Further along the Mana road was Nouveau camp, used for incurable prisoners who had been released from the hospital and sent into the jungle to die. Men suffering from every sort of tropical disease were kept in a series of long huts where their condition worsened very rapidly from bad food and neglect. The doctor from St. Laurent visited the camp every week, but there was little he could do.

Major Charles Pean of the Salvation Army, on a tour of the penal colony in 1928, described his visit to Nouveau camp.

"...I took my place in the bush "taxi" and were set off toward Nouveau camp, which at a distance looked rather inviting. The white thatched huts, the wells and the kitchen garden reminded me of a gay colonial farm. Alas, the mask soon fell and the hideous face of the convict settlement stood revealed. We were spared none of its blemishes. Greater misery than this could hardly be imagined. Here was the anteroom to the grave, a gateway to hell. Here two hundred and sixty men were dying, if such a word may be used to describe these beings who were eaten through and through with disease.

"Two of the huts resounded with the throaty rattle of consumptives whose waxen faces, drained of all color, were contorted by each successive paroxysm of coughing. Farther along was the hut containing the cripples, the armless, the legless, who lying around all day passed the time in an exchange of obscenities.

"In yet another hut were more dying men. Stretched out on their foul straw mattresses were paralytics, disfigured syphilitics and one man with cancer of the face, but without any bandages to cover his running sores..."

Before World War I, the most dreaded camp in Guiana was Orapu. Located seventy miles from Cayenne in dense jungle, a convict poet who lived and died there composed the frightening prison song named for this camp. Convicts held in the blockhaus frequently sang it the night before an execution, and thus it was passed down through the generations of prisoners. "Cry, cry for yourselves," it went, "your hearts beat no longer."

Often repeated in popular accounts of the penal colony, although not totally verifiable, is the story of Melino and Yvon. Before chains were abolished and convicts were attached in pairs at the ankle, two men, Melino and Yvon, arrived at Orapu. They were known enemies, so the guards chained them together, as was customary to lessen the chance of escape.

After several weeks together, Melino and Yvon escaped from the camp and headed through the bush toward the interior gold mines. They hoped that in the gold camp the prospectors would cut the metal chains that held them together. For eight days they trekked through thick jungle, chased by guards from Orapu. On the ninth day, stopping to rest near a small creek, Melino grabbed a tree branch to keep his balance. In doing so he disturbed a small but deadly viper which struck him before he could move his hand out of the way. It bit him above the wrist, injecting a full dose of venom.

The bite of the tree viper caused a slow and painful death. Yvon, still chained to Melino, stood by helplessly as his companion writhed in agony for several hours. At last, Melino's body gave one last convulsion and was still. Yvon, now lost in the jungle without supplies, was chained to a corpse. For several hours he tried frantically to cut the dead man's foot off and free himself of the corpse, but this proved impossible. Finally he gave up and fell asleep under a large tree.

He awoke the next morning to the frightening discovery that rodents had nipped the toes off the feet of his dead chain-mate. Realizing that his escape was doomed, his only wish was to find his way back to Orapu and be rid of this corpse appendage.

The chain that linked the live and dead man together had enough play that Yvon could carry the corpse on his back while he tramped through the dense vegetation. But the camp was several days away and the body decomposed rapidly in the jungle humidity. The reek of the corpse attracted a swarm of insects, and vultures began flying overhead.

When Yvon made it back to Orapu on the fourteenth day of his escape, the corpse was detached and he was sent to the hospital. He never regained sanity after the episode and died exhausted the next year. He was never able to sleep for more than a few minutes before waking up screaming. The nightmare of his ordeal in the bush kept returning.

Horror stories like this didn't occur every day in the bagne, but during the century of the penal colony tragedies took place that were never forgotten. Convicts who attempted to flee through the jungle without supplies met with disaster more often than not. Besides malaria and snakes, some escapers met up with other prisoners on the run who were desperate, violent and sometimes insane.

In 1931, another macabre drama unfolded in the bush, this time near the convict camp at Gourdonville. Located twenty miles up the Kourou river and surrounded by jungle, the camp was originally a small gold mining station. It was still small — only fifty convicts at a time worked there making boards and beams from trees cut in the vicinity. No guards were stationed there. There was no need as the camp was surrounded by jungle. Every fifteen days a canoe arrived with supplies, and a guard who left the same day called the convict roll. A small boat came once a week to pick up the camp's production and take away sick prisoners.

It was one of the easier camps and the quota set by the guards was not excessive. Most could complete their work in several days and spend the next two-week period hunting butterflies or collecting rubber from trees in the bush. If a man could stay healthy — that is, not collapse from fever — he could make a great deal of money at this camp. At the end of the two weeks, the guards bought all the butterflies and rubber from the convicts at a fair price. But most convicts came down with fever and lasted just a few months there.

Two convicts who had been at Gourdonville the longest, almost a year, requested permission to return to Kourou when the next supply boat arrived. On August 15th when the boat arrived, the two convicts were gone. The guards thought it strange that they would escape after requesting a transfer. A small search was mounted and when a day of looking for them in the jungle produced no trace, the guards wrote a report to St. Laurent listing the two as missing. They were put on the roster of escaped prisoners and duly forgotten.

Several months later a solitary gold prospector trekking through the forest made a horrifying discovery. About twenty miles from Gourdonville he came across a huge red ant nest several feet in height. On each side of the ant hill a wooden stake had been driven into the ground; tied to the stakes by liana vines were the arm and leg bones of two men. The rest of the skeletons stood up straight from within the ant nest. A few tattered shreds of fabric clinging to the place where the limbs had been tied were clearly the thin red and white cotton of the convict uniform.

Rumor has it that the two convicts were working in the forest, and came across a band of escaped prisoners who had heard of their transfer request. It was well known that these two men were wealthy, by convict standards, from butterfly collecting. They had been tied to the ant hill to make them turn over their money. But they had no cash on them for all their savings were held by a Chinese shopkeeper in Cayenne, hence their transfer request. They had been planning to collect their money in Cayenne and then escape from there to Brazil. When their tormentors realized that the two had no money on them, they left them in disgust to be eaten alive by the ants.

The largest and bloodiest convict gang to roam the jungle was composed of ten Arab convicts. They escaped from the road-building camp at Kourou and terrorized isolated farms in the interior for two years. These Arabs seemed well adapted to the jungle, and they went from hamlet to hamlet raping and stealing, killing anyone who was unfortunate enough to cross them. They attacked isolated huts and carried off food and weapons. When it became known that they were armed with rifles taken in an attack on a hunter's home, panic began to spread through the Creole villages along the coast.

An expedition of guards and police, accompanied by bush-negro hunters, went into the jungle to capture the Arabs. They were not successful. Each day they would find some trace of the fugitives and each night they returned to their camp empty-handed. Several times they came across smoldering fire of the Arabs' latest camp. They were only a day behind, but a day is like a month in the bush where dense vegetation hides everything.

After four months of searching, the guards and police gave up and the massacres continued, this time in villages near the Brazilian border. The Arabs knew that they would soon have to flee the colony. They had already killed a guard from the Cayenne prison who stumbled upon them. And the villagers in isolated huts in the interior were now protecting themselves and firing back when the Arabs came to attack.

In September of 1934, five members of the band were surprised and captured in an isolated clearing thirty miles from Kourou. Several weeks later, three more were taken by Indians as they prepared to cross the Oyapock river into Brazil. All of them were brought back to St. Laurent under heavy guard (the civilians were roused and wanted to kill them). They appeared before the T.M.S. of 1935. Six were sentenced to death, three of them were guillotined later that year by La Durelle. This was one of the only executions (along with that of Hespel, the old executioner) that was cheered by the convicts in St. Laurent. The Arabs had robbed and killed several escaped prisoners during their reign of terror.

And their decapitation was well remembered. At the crack of dawn Najid, Ahmed and Khalib were moved from their death row cells into the courtyard where the guillotine was set up. The head guard read their sentences aloud and declared that their appeals had been rejected. He asked each of the condemned men if they wanted to pray. "No," each responded. "Would you like a last cigarette?," he offered. "No," they barked. The chief guard then asked if they had anything to say. "Yes," they replied in unison, "Drop dead, you filthy bastard."

And with that the three were lined up, and their heads chopped off.

For reasons that have never been clear, their heads were not buried with the bodies, but were kept in preserving solution in jars along with several other guillotined heads. These jars were kept in a basement room of the Jean Martial hospital in Cayenne in a display case (some have claimed that they were kept there until as late as 1970) until the heads were finally removed and buried on the outskirts of town.

The road-building camp at Kourou which the Arabs had escaped from was perhaps the most ambitious project of the penal colony. It was also the bagne's biggest fiasco. It was an attempt to link the entire coast of French Guiana by road — from Brazil to Surinam. Any chance for the colony to develop was hindered by the fact that the coastal towns were far apart, linked only by infrequent boat service. No goods could cross the coast; it was jungle and swamp.

Today, nearly a century later, this road is still to be completed.

Work was begun on the highway in 1906, with Macouria outside Cayenne as the starting point. Officially called "Route Number One" it soon became known as "Route Zero" to the convicts who worked on it. By 1923, the year of Albert Londre's visit, only twenty-four kilometers had been completed. Only twenty-four kilometers in nearly twenty years. And it cost thousands of lives.

"We arrive at kilometer twenty-four," Londres wrote, "it's the end of the world.

"And for the first time I see the bagne.

"There are one hundred men there, all of them sick with a stomach ailment. Some standing, some lying and groaning in pain.

"The bush is in front of them resembling a wall. But it's not they who will break the wall down, it's the wall that will break them.

"This is not a work camp, it's a cistern well-hidden in French Guiana's forest where they throw men who will never get up again.

"Therefore, the question is whether this is a project to build a road or a project to kill convicts. If it's a project to kill convicts, don't change anything. All goes well..."

The mortality on this road was alarming. Figures as high as 17,000 deaths have been claimed, although this is an exaggeration. The exact number is impossible to calculate. It must be remembered that this was *not* a punishment camp. The convicts who went to Kourou were classified as "fit for road work". They didn't stay that way very long.

Conditions on this road project were aggravated by the fact that officials sold much of the equipment necessary to build the road to Dutch farmers across the river in Surinam. The guards posted in Kourou were a frustrated and brutal lot, afflicted with malaria and annoyed that they had been given such a desolate posting.

After the First World War it was mainly Arab convicts who were sent to work on the road. It was thought that Europeans could not survive this kind of work. The Arabs, however, did not fare much better. Even with quinine available to combat malaria, the death rate remained the same.

The project reached the thirty-six kilometer point before it was abandoned. After years of work and thousands of deaths, it was a road that went from nowhere to nowhere. It was not until 1955 that St. Laurent and Cayenne were linked by road.

In 1930, the colony of French Guiana was reduced by decree to a small strip of land on the the coast, ten percent of its original area. The vast Territory of Innini was created from the remaining area. Innini was under the direct control of a Governor and had no elected officials. It was established as a result of the huge scandals involving local politicians and their activity in business schemes in the interior. The final straw was the murder of Jean Galmot in Cayenne two years before. Galmot, a Frenchman, was very popular among the Creoles and was running for the office of député of French Guiana at that time.

This move reflected the reality of Guiana at that time as well as today. The interior territory was inhabited by primitive Indians and gold miners. Innini's populace had little to do with the colony's life in and around Cayenne. The new territory lifted authority from Cayenne and permitted the French government to collect taxes from the gold mines and protect the Indians from abuse by Creole politicians and their business schemes.

When Innini was created, the French empire stretched to all corners of the globe with colonial holdings in Indochina comprising what is now Vietnam, Cambodia and Laos. On paper these colonies had control of their internal affairs, but the reality was quite different. Colonial bureaucrats and French businessmen took actual power away from traditional war-lords. Anti-colonialist sentiment spread among certain elements of the population and isolated rebellions flared up. Terrorist attacks were countered with French military force.

In 1925, to consolidate power in Indo-China, France officially lifted local control and tension began to mount. Alexandre Varenne, the area's French governor, kept the situation under control by calming diverse nationalist factions, preventing large-scale revolt.

But Varennes' term as Governor expired and he left for France in 1928. The shaky peace that he had held together began to unravel. On February 10th, 1930, nationalist soldiers from the colonial garrison at Yen Bay revolted. Several French officers were killed and the rebellion spread to the streets of Hanoi, where some of the soldiers threw small bombs made from sardine tins at the bastions of French authority.

It did not lead to a full-scale revolution. The political factions were not unified and hundreds of the rebels were arrested and thrown into the infamous concentration prison at Paulo Condor.

French authorities were not happy with keeping potential subversives anywhere in Indo-China. The new Governor had the authority to send "undesirables" and political convicts to any colonial territory, and decided to do so. Innini was chosen, and 600 of the rebels arrived in French Guiana in February 1931.

These Indo-Chinese convicts were not under the direct control of the penal administration, which was the force of law in the rest of the convict camps. They were commanded by a special prison service created solely for their incarceration.

On arrival the Indo-Chinese convicts were kept for a short time at the abandoned convict camp on Creek Spourine to await assignment. By the end of the year it was decided that they would set to building roads to open up the interior.

Camp Forestiere opened in 1931. It lay on the Maroni River, twenty miles from St. Jean on the border of Guiana and Innini. Work on a road between the camp and St. Jean never got very far. It took nearly three years to clear and establish the base camp and when road work finally began in 1933, the camp was closed for reasons of bad sanitation.

Creek Anguille opened the same year as Foresteire. It was created as another camp for the Indo-Chinese convicts, situated twenty-five miles from Cayenne. The proposed road through the jungle to Cayenne encountered the same problems as at Foresteire. It took years to get the camp into operation and by the time work finally began, the men were all sick. Sanitary conditions were so bad, and death by snake bite so common, that in 1937 most of the 350 inmates went on a hunger strike. Three died as a result.

Still, conditions didn't change, and fifteen inmates made an all-night march to Cayenne to camp in front of the Governor's residence in protest. They demanded to talk with the colony's highest official but to no avail. The Indo-Chinese were arrested for escape and sentenced to solitary confinement.

A third camp for Indo-Chinese convicts fared little better than Forestiere or Creek Anguille. Opened in 1933, Saut Tigre, located on the Sinnimary river, was created to build a road through the interior, to link Cayenne and St. Laurent by way of the paths that had linked the interior gold camps. Some of the convicts who had been at Forestiere were transferred to Saut Tigre, but the road project was abandoned in 1937 when mortality rates surpassed those of even Creek Anguille.

A 1939 decree pardoned the survivors of the Yen Bay revolt and eighty returned to Indo-China that year. But the remaining men would have to wait until 1954 to return home. World War II blocked shipping lanes, and then the French War in Vietnam made it impossible for the authorities to allow the return of former rebels.

A dozen remained in French Guiana voluntarily and opened restaurants in the coastal village. The camps where they toiled trying to scratch roads through the jungle were abandoned. The solitary confinement cells still remain in the midst of overgrown vegetation.

ESCAPE

Scattered through the annals of many South American and Caribbean republics are accounts of the flimsy crafts which washed onto their beaches. The ragged, bearded, thirst-parched men who stumbled from them, more dead than alive, had escaped from Guiana. They had spent weeks on the open seas in leaky boats — if the dugout canoes of the Maroni could be called boats.

Their exact number will never be known. Those fortunate enough to find a deserted inlet made their way to the nearest big town and quietly built new lives. The less fortunate fell into the arms of the local police. Some managed to escape extradition. Others found their excursion short-lived, and were given "return tickets" to the solitary confinement cells on St. Joseph.

And there is no record of how many canoes with patchwork sails overturned during a tropical storm, leaving their "sailors" hoping to drown before the sharks came around for breakfast. No one was there to count the corpses reduced to skeletons by red ants and vultures in the middle of the jungle. When a sick and hungry man drops in the forest, all evidence quickly disappears.

The number of convicts captured, returned, discovered dead, or whose whereabouts were known, but extradition attempts had failed, added to the number who gave themselves up provides a figure well below the number of total escapes. It is impossible to trace the fates of all those unaccounted for. Whether a prisoner died the day of his escape under the first big wave he encountered at sea, or if he went on to run a brothel somewhere in Peru cannot be known with any great accuracy. Those who made it to freedom normally didn't advertise their origins.

During the 1920's and 30's, there is no doubt that hundreds of them were living throughout Latin America under false names. To those who came across them (usually in the red light districts) and knew their real identity, they were known as the Maroni boys or the Cayenne gang. They came to the notice of the underworld and the local police, as they got involved in local vice rackets, and occasionally in narcotics trafficking.

For all its dangers an escape by sea seemed to offer the best, if not the only chance of success. An overland trek through the forest was a journey from nowhere to nowhere. It was easy enough to flee the convict camps. Many of the men at St. Laurent and Cayenne had a free run of the town, reporting only twice a day to the barracks. The houseboys employed by civilians often slept outside the camp and libérés reported to the police only twice a year.

In order to avoid eventual recapture, any man escaping the bagne had to get out of the colony and settle in a country which would not send him back. To do this required a boat, simple navigation equipment, food supplies and trustworthy companions. Escape by sea couldn't be attempted alone and failure would mean a horrible death, or several years on St. Joseph if sent back to French Guiana.

To be considered "escaped" by the prison administration meant absence for at least twelve hours from the last roll call. A convict captured before the twelve hour limit was charged with "illegal absence" and punished less severely.

There was a vast number of escapes on record since nearly every convict tried once and many tried several times. Officially the figure passed 50,000 during the century of the penal colony's existence, but of that number only fifteen percent never returned to French Guiana.

The great majority of escapees were either captured inside French Guiana or sent back from neighboring countries. Some gave themselves up voluntarily after weeks or months in the jungle, living like rats and half-eaten by parasites. In 1923, official records indicate 243 non-returned escapees out of a total of nearly 800 who tried. This was the largest number for any year according to official records, but events the following year would make escape more difficult.

Before 1924, Surinam was the popular destination for all those who wished to flee the colony. The Dutch authorities did not consistently send back escaped convicts, and many found work at the American-run bauxite mines near Moengo, fifty miles from the Maroni river. For convicts at St. Laurent, this meant that crossing the river and following jungle paths to Moengo might result in temporary refuge. Skilled workmen were needed, and well paid. If a convict was valuable to the mine, the local police looked the other way so long as he didn't cause trouble.

But few escapees intended to stay in Surinam. They worked at Moengo until they had enough money to continue on to Venezuela or Columbia. The Dutch police had a habit of rounding up escapees and sending them back to St. Laurent whenever the mine slowed down and laid off workers.

Then in early 1924, a crime was committed which so enraged the Dutch that from then on, the doors of Surinam were closed to convicts escaping from French Guiana. The French convicts were now feared by the local populace.

Marcel Coutancot worked as a laborer on a small plantation near Moengo. He had escaped from the bagne several years before and married a local girl from Surinam.

One Sunday Coutancot began a drinking spree and broke into the shop of a Chinese trader. He demanded tafia, but had no money. When the shopkeeper refused him, Coutancot pulled a bottle from the shelf and broke it over the man's head. As the body crashed to the floor, Coutancot took a jerrycan filled with kerosene and poured it over the injured man and throughout the rest of the shop. He struck a match and staggered out of the shop with several bottles of rum. The shopkeeper was burned alive with his wife and daughter who were trapped in a back room.

Taken to Paramaribo under heavy guard (villagers from Moengo wanted to lynch him), Coutancot was tried for triple murder and hung later that year. By decree of Queen Wilhemina, the Dutch police, supported by the local populace, rounded up all of the escaped Guiana prisoners and sent them back to St. Laurent. Some had been in Surinam for more than a decade, but it made no difference. From that moment on, any convict from the bagne found in Surinam was immediately returned.

There was one exception. German convicts who escaped to Surinam were brought to Paramaribo to be questioned by the German consul. If the consul was satisfied as to their identity — which involved an extensive interrogation and a response from Berlin — the man was given free passage back to Germany. Records indicate that the German Embassy in Paris was active in pressing the French government to pardon or commute the sentences of German nationals. After release the German consul in Paramaribo arranged free passage back to Germany.

Not many Germans were sent to Guiana as prisoners — perhaps fifty at any one time. Word soon got out that the Dutch would not send Germans back, and the French began keeping most of the Germans on the islands or in Cayenne where escape to Surinam would not be so easy. Many non-French convicts claimed to be German when caught in Surinam — but it didn't work. The German consul was never fooled when a Dane or a Pole tried to pass himself off as German, and the man was sent back to the bagne very quickly.

A minority of convicts and relégués were not French, but foreigners convicted in France or in the French Foreign Legion. In 1916, the relégué camp at St. Jean boasted eighteen Germans, twenty-four Belgians, twenty-four Italians, six English and Americans (the distinction was not made) and a handful of other Europeans among the more than 2,000 Frenchmen in the camp. There were more foreigners in the convict camps.

The foreigners tended to stick together. Some didn't speak a word of French when they left for Guiana, but all would learn quickly since the guards had little patience if a man didn't understand a command. And they often stuck together while escaping. When Henri Bauve fled the bagne in 1933, he was accompanied by a Russian, three Poles and an Italian.

Escapes from the relégué camp at St. Jean were even more frequent than in the convict camps but fewer actually succeeded. Exactly 15,895 relégués were sent to Guiana and over 20,000 attempted escapes occurred. Relégués prepared their escapes in a much clumsier manner than transportés. Perhaps it was because they were generally less intelligent, but more likely they had less to fear if captured. Since they were legally free men and retained their civil rights, the maximum penalty for escape was thirty days solitary confinement. They gave themselves up at the first sign of trouble, while a convict would hide in the bush since several years in solitary confinement awaited him if recaptured. Interrogations of relégués were always the same:

Question: From where did you escape?
Answer: St. Jean du Maroni.
Question: Did you have any money?
Answer: No.
Question: Did you have supplies?
Answer: No.
Question: How were you caught?
Answer: I gave myself up when I couldn't find any food.

Most convicts serving time in Cayenne and Kourou tried to escape to Brazil. The official Brazilian policy was to send French Guiana convicts back, but it is a big country, one where a man could easily disappear. And communication and cooperation between the police forces of the different Brazilian states was not always favorable. Only when the French consul made strong extradition requests to local authorities would Brazilian police detain convicts for return to Guiana.

The border towns on the east side of the Oyapock river didn't attract many escapees. Most headed as quickly as possible to Belem, 500 miles from Cayenne. It wasn't easy to get to. There were no roads and very few villages. The jungle became even denser as the forest neared the Amazon river. The only way to Belem was by boat.

As in St. Laurent, obtaining a boat depended on having sufficient funds. The Chinese sold boats to escaping convicts, and never informed the guards of the convict's plans. The bush-negroes also constructed and sold canoes which could stand a sea voyage. And there were civilians who would take escaping convicts in their fishing boats and drop them off in Brazil, or Brazilian smugglers hoping to make a few extra francs. But they had a bad reputation.

The story of the package escape agent was often told in various versions. Victor Bichier-Desages was a French Guianese fisherman. The father of three children, most of his time was spent at sea off the coast of Guiana. He went to Cayenne periodically to sell his catch and it was rumored that, for a price, he would take escaping convicts with him and drop them off in a small hamlet near the Brazilian border.

In February 1918, Mr. Emelien Polycarpe, resident of the isolated village of Kaw, was taking his boat down the Kaw river when he heard human cries coming from the left bank. It was near the sea in a swamp and mangrove-covered part of the coast. As he neared the bank, a badly wounded man rushed toward his craft. The man, an Arab convict, had bullet wounds on his head and buttocks. Polycarpe brought the half-dead man on board and made for Cayenne. The Arab had been in the swamps for two days.

In Cayenne the convict, when brought before the police, admitted escaping from a detail of prisoners installing telegraph wires near Macouria. He had fled with four other convicts, and told the police in detail about their escape.

The leader, an Arab libéré named Ben Hoummada, contacted the fisherman Bichier-Desage a week before and arranged for him to pick them up at a deserted spot on the coast near the village of Tonate, twenty miles west of Cayenne. Bichier was to carry them to the Brazilian border for 500 francs each.

Several nights later, the four convicts broke out of their camp as planned and found Ben Hoummada at the prearranged spot. Within hours, the hurricane lantern of a boat broke the inky blackness of night and approached to within feet of shore. It was Bichier and his mate Apollinaire. After turning over 2,500 francs to Bichier, the five convicts climbed aboard and the boat headed west toward Brazil.

Early the next morning, having passed Cayenne in the night, Bichier brought the boat within several hundred feet of the coast and dropped anchor. He told the escaping convicts that having sailed all night, he was tired and wanted to sleep for several hours before continuing towards Brazil in the afternoon. Suspecting nothing, the convicts stretched out on deck and slept.

Early in the afternoon, one of the convicts awoke and discovered that the tide was nearly a mile out. The boat was sitting in several feet of soft mud. Paying little attention to the convicts on board, Appolinaire jumped off the boat into the mud and lay belly-down on a piece of drift wood. By paddling with his hands and feet he made it to the tree-line in several minutes. The escaping convicts started asking what was going on. Saying nothing, Bichier grabbed his hunting rifle and ammunition pouch. He jumped into the mud as Appolinaire had done and started off on another piece of drift wood toward the jungle.

When he was thirty feet from the boat, Bichier stopped, turned around and faced the boat. He steadied himself on the drift wood and aimed his rifle at the Arabs in the boat.

Firing rapidly, he literally blew off two of the Arabs' heads. Two others fell and died seconds later. Only one of the escaping convicts managed to jump off the boat into the mud. Though wounded he made it to the trees; Bichier had no rounds left to fire. Fearing Bichier was going to follow him into the swamps to finish the job, the Arab waited for an entire day in the mangroves before moving on.

However, Bichier returned to the boat and spread out the four corpses in a row on the deck. After searching his victims' clothing, he took out his fishing knife and began his work. Slitting their bellies, he reached into the intestines and bowels of the dead Arabs and extracted their plans. Pocketing the contents, he yelled out to Apollinaire standing on the beach to return to the boat.

Hours later, the tide came in and they headed off to sea. Many miles from the coast that night, the bodies were dumped overboard and the deck washed of blood and brain tissue. The two men continued their fishing trip.

Having heard rumors of this incident, the police arrested Bichier and Apollinaire and placed them in detention. Bichier denied everything but Apollinaire finally broke under questioning and admitted what had happened, filling in the police about the disemboweling. He died several days later without revealing how many of other men Bichier had killed over the years.

Bichier was brought to trial in Cayenne and sentenced to twenty years at hard labor. He was sent to Ile Royale, where all native French Guianese prisoners were held. Ironically, after three years he was made a turnkey — one who guarded and chased convicts who tried to escape.

Even more horrible than the Bichier massacre was the escape by the Longueville brothers, whose break for freedom turned to cannibalism.

Marcel and Dedé Longueville were terrors in the penal colony. Both stood over six feet and were covered with tattoos. Natives of Algeria, they has spent years in Biribi and had emerged in Guiana as feared fort-à-bras.

The Longueville brothers had taken great pains to ensure the success of their escape. They had paid over 3,000 francs for the boat which was well-equipped and stocked for a long sea voyage since they hoped to make it as far as Cuba. Three others had also paid for a place in the boat, an Italian named Gaston and a fort-à-bras/môme couple from Paris. A sixth man, Jean-Marie, a Breton who claimed to have served in the navy, was taken along without having to pay. This was the usual arrangement for "navigators" whose skills the escape depended upon. They left St. Laurent one night at the end of 1922, and headed toward the Maroni. Dedé Longueville uttered this warning to the Breton: "We trust you and you're welcome to come along without paying, but screw up and you'll pay dearly!"

At ten o'clock that night, the six escapees paddled silently down river and within hours were passing Point Hattes, where the Maroni and the Atlantic Ocean meet. It was well done; they hadn't attracted the attention of the guards stationed there.

The sea for the first several miles off the Guiana coast where the Maroni empties is very dangerous. It has been called 'the Frenchmen's graveyard,' since sand bars extend for miles and crafts caught in them are trapped in the soft mud. At the helm the Breton quickly made an error in judgement. Instead of taking the boat far enough away from the coast, he turned the canoe west too soon and within hours the boat was stuck on the Dutch coast.

Enraged by the mistake, a snarling Dedé Longueville ordered everyone out of the boat and the Breton knew that his time was up. "I told you that you would pay dearly if you tricked us into believing you were a sailor!" Dedé Longueville screamed. "On your knees you bastard!"

The Breton begged for forgiveness, but Dedé responded by pulling out his knife and stabbing the Breton several times in the chest. With a grunt he withdrew his blade and wiped the blood on the Breton's trousers.

The two Parisians and Gaston trembled with fear, while Marcel Longueville rolled the body over and dragged it a few feet away. They were stuck in front of a large swamp with mangrove and quicksand separating the coast from the jungle.

For two days the group, now five, huddled together on the coast and were attacked by waves of mosquitos. They had nothing to eat, their food supply having washed

Convicts boarding a prison ship bound for French
Guiana, 1930s. AP/WIDE WORLD PHOTO

Devil's Island as seen from Ile Royale.   ALEXANDER MILES PHOTO

Prisoners of the penal colony showing their elaborate homemade tattoos. AP/WIDE WORLD PHOTO

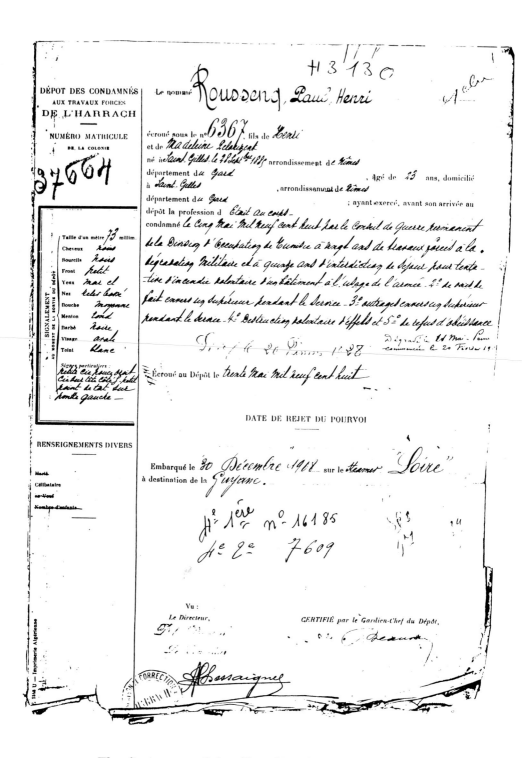

The first page of the file of Paul Henri Roussenq,
king of the dark cells. COURTESY CENTRE DES ARCHIVES D'OUTRE-MER

Above: A prisoner chained to his workplace by welded-on leg irons. VANGUARD PRESS, INC.

Below: A *plan*; device used by prisoners to conceal money for escape. DRAWING BY J. McVey

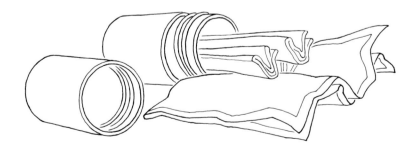

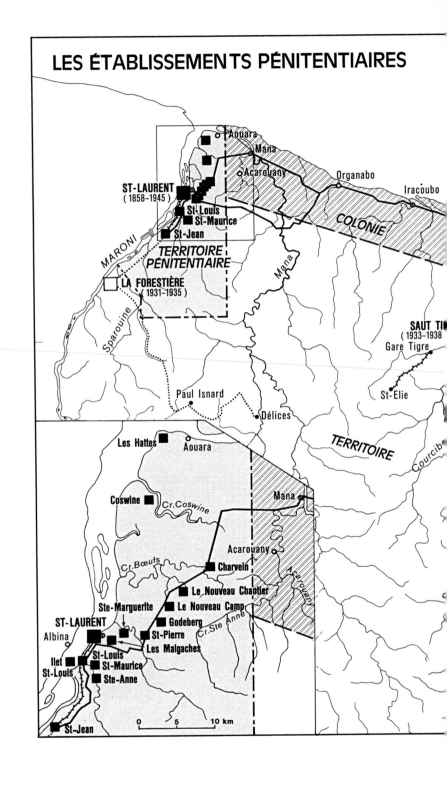

LES ÉTABLISSEMENTS PÉNITENTIAIRES

Aouara
Mana
Acarouany
Organabo
Iracoubo

ST-LAURENT
(1858-1945)

St-Louis
St-Maurice
St-Jean

COLONIE

MARONI

Mana

TERRITOIRE
PÉNITENTIAIRE

LA FORESTIÈRE
(1931-1935)

Sparouine

SAUT TI
(1933-1938
Gare Tigre

Paul Isnard

Délices

St-Elie

TERRITOIRE

Courcib

Les Hattes
Aouara

Coswine
Cr.Coswine

Mana

Acarouany

Cr.Bœufs

Charvein

Le Nouveau Chantier

Ste-Marguerite
Le Nouveau Camp

ST-LAURENT
Godeberg
Albina
St-Pierre
Cr.Ste-Anne
St-Louis
Les Malgaches
Ilet
St-Maurice
St-Louis
Ste-Anne

St-Jean

0   5   10 km

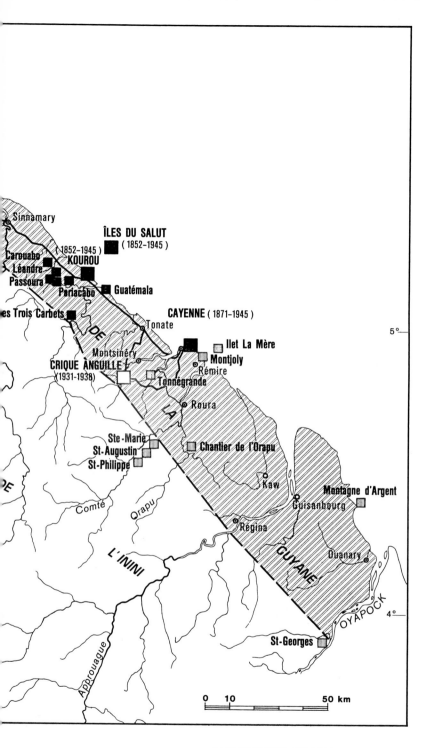

Sinnamary

ÎLES DU SALUT
(1852–1945)

Carouabo
Léandre
Passoura
(1852–1945)
KOUROU

Pariacabo
Guatémala

es Trois Carbets

CAYENNE (1871–1945)

Tonate

5°

Ilet La Mère

Montsinéry

CRIQUE ANGUILLE
(1931–1938)

Montjoly

Rémire

Tonnégrande

Roura

Ste-Marie
St-Augustin
St-Philippe

Chantier de l'Orapu

Kaw

Montagne d'Argent

Comté

Orapu

Guisanbourg

L'ININI

DE LA GUYANE

Régina

Ouanary

4°

OYAPOCK

St-Georges

Approuague

0   10   50 km

MAP COURTESY OF EMILE ABONNENC

Captain Alfred Dreyfus

Guillaume Seznec

Collection of preserved severed heads from the penal
colony. PHOTO COURTESY OF LUCIE MARIE MADELEINE VAUDÉ

The Camp de la Transportation as it is today.
ALEXANDER MILES PHOTO

Henri Bauve and Lucien Bellouard in 1982, two prisoners who decide to stay in Guiana after the penal colony's dissolution. ALEXANDER MILES PHOTO

The ruins of Blockhaus No. 1 at St. Laurent, where prisoners were held before trial. ALEXANDER MILES PHOTO

The last remains of the penal colony are being slowly reclaimed by the jungle. ALEXANDER MILES PHOTO

overboard in the waves before they landed. Only small crabs were edible and few could be found.

On the third morning, the Longueville brothers decided to send the Parisians into the swamps to look for a trail that might lead to an Indian village. They were to return the next morning and rejoin Gaston and the Longueville brothers who would wait on the coast. The Parisians had no choice; after what had happened to the Breton, they were not going to refuse the Longuevilles.

The next morning only one of the Parisians returned. It was the fort-à-bras Pascal, and he was wearing one of the môme's shoes. "Where is the little one?" demanded Dédé Longueville. Pascal said that they had split up the night before. The môme had disappeared, and Pascal returned to the coast without him hoping that he would find his own way back.

The Longueville brothers were terribly hungry and doubted Pascal's story. Nevertheless, they grabbed their machetes and went into the swamp with Pascal in hopes of finding the môme. Pascal didn't seem as weak as the others, but acted as though he was upset over the disappearance of his "friend."

"You, Gaston, stay here and look for crabs while we go and find the môme," ordered the Longuevilles as they headed off into the swamps.

They headed off with a seemingly nervous Pascal in front and the Longuevilles several feet behind. They hadn't gone far when they made their discovery. Three miles from the coast, the Longueville brothers came upon a horrible sight. In back of a large mud hill, hidden in the mangroves, lay a human body. Dédé Longueville ordered Pascal to stay where he was while his brother Marcel went to take a look.

It was the body of the môme, scarred with horrible knife wounds. It was mutilated in many places and the buttocks had been sliced off.

Screaming with rage, the Longueville brothers brought Pascal to the body and forced him to stare at his dead "friend," saying "You bastard, you killed him to eat him, you have no shame."

Pascal was now in tears. "Forgive me," he cried, "the boy couldn't walk any longer and I was so hungry."

Now it was Marcel Longueville who pulled his knife. There was nothing to say. Pascal killed his môme to eat him and now he would die for the act. Only one thrust was made in the throat, and Pascal gurgled and choked on blood before he died.

The body was dragged to the coast where Gaston was waiting. He hadn't found many crabs and soon dusk would fall. None of the three men had eaten for two days.

As night fell the Longueville brothers went to work. With a butcher's calm, they laid Pascal's body down on the sand and in twenty minutes his legs, thighs and buttocks were neatly sliced into filets. They made a fire of dried drift wood, cooked the steaks over the coals and ate lustily. The blood was boiled and drunk, and what they hadn't eaten was salted and put into their kit bags. "We'll be hungry tomorrow," grunted Marcel Longueville.

The next morning all traces of the body were buried in the sand and the three men headed off into the swamps. In several hours they found a small trail, and by afternoon walked straight into an Indian village.

At first the Indians welcomed the three escaped convicts into the village, and prepared a meal of fish and cassava for them. As they ate, the village chief began to suspect something. He had come across escaping convicts before, and ordered them to open their kit bags. Surrounded by thirty Indians with machetes, the Longueville brothers had no choice. The bags were opened and their grisly contents revealed. The three convicts were chased out of the village at once and into the jungle. The Indians had only revulsion for cannibalism.

Within days the three were arrested by Dutch police-men and sent back to St. Laurent. The Longueville brothers kept quiet, but Gaston couldn't keep his mouth shut. Soon everyone in St. Laurent heard of the horrible events.

But nothing could be proved. The killings had taken place in Dutch territory and the French had no jurisdiction. The T.M.S. sentenced the three to solitary confinement for escape only.

More successful was the escape of Eugene Dieudonné, a minor figure in the anarchist Bonnot Gang that terrorized France before the First World War. Dieudonné was con-demned to death but given a reprieve at the last moment by President Raymond Poincaré. Poincaré had doubts about Dieudonné's guilt in an anarchist attack in 1911, during which two policemen were killed. Dieudonné's sentence was commuted to life at hard labor in Guiana.

For fifteen years, Dieudonné wore the red and white striped convict uniform in St. Laurent and on the islands. His two escape attempts ended in recapture; the second, to Venezuela, earned him two years in solitary confinement on St. Joseph.

In 1926, he was sent to Cayenne and took up his old trade of cabinet maker, enjoying a free run of the town. In December of that year, Dieudonné arranged to flee the penal colony with two others on a Brazilian boat out of Cayenne. The Captain was to pass the border and drop the three off on the coast.

But sailing against the current proved too difficult for the Captain, and the boat slammed into the French coast. Marooned, the convicts took off into the jungle, and after a month of wandering, miraculously found and crossed the Oyapock river into Brazil.

The border towns were no refuge, so Dieudonné and his two companions headed to Belem; two months later they arrived there at the height of carnival. It was lucky for them, since their appearance after two months in the bush and on the coastal tramp ships would have normally attracted the attention of Belem's police. But now they were assumed to be men dressed as hobos for the festivities.

Richard, one of the escapers, was seriously ill from the two month trek so the other two searched the town for the Catholic hospital. They carried the sick man through the streets, his tattooed figure shaking with malaria.

It was a French nurse who received them and she immediately understood. "Another one! " she exclaimed, upon seeing the French tattoo inscriptions on Richard's dying body. She knew where they came from.

The next day Richard was dead and within a week, Dieudonne and his companion found work near the town's waterfront. Under assumed names, the two rented a room and lived quietly for several months.

Eventually their luck ran out. They were arrested and put in detention for extradition to Cayenne. The companion was soon sent back to Guiana, but Dieudonné's case proved more complicated.

It had been more than fifteen years since the Bonnot Gang's activities had made headlines throughout Europe. They had been forgotten by the public but not by the police, and even the Brazilians had heard of them. Dieudonné, though not the ringleader, had been a famous man. Only he, of the four men convicted, escaped the guillotine.

Belem is the capital of Para, Brazil's the northern-most state. Para's chief of police held Dieudonné in custody despite extradition requests from the French consul, ordered by the Ministry of Justice in Paris. He began looking into the Dieudonné case and came to doubt the fairness of the conviction. It was not under his jurisdiction to question the merits of French justice and the guilt or innocence of a man convicted more than fifteen years before — but he was deeply moved by Dieudonné's claim of a frame-up.

When it became known that Dieudonné was being held in Para, the chief of police in the state of Pernambuco, an arch-enemy of the police chief of Para, stepped in and publicly called for Dieudonné's return to French Guiana. He would do anything to discredit his counterpart in Para. The affair became a national and international incident and a press campaign in Brazil and France ensued. Dieudonné's case was widely discussed and there were claims that France was guilty of a miscarriage of justice. Sensitive to public opinion, the Brazilian Minister of Justice demanded that Dieudonné be sent to Rio de Janiero, since he wanted to meet him personally before deciding on extradition. It was a break with international custom, but officials saw that Dieudonné was becoming an international symbol; it would be politically harmful to send him back on the first boat.

Instead, Eugene Dieudonné, serving a life sentence under French law, embarked on a first class cruise from Belem to Rio. At each port of call, reporters were waiting at the dock to interview him and his arrival in Rio was a front-page story.

In France, the Dieudonné affair was also causing a great deal of controversy. Not wishing to add fuel to a already growing international fire, and at the same time not wishing to admit to judicial error, the French Ministry of Justice began to look into the facts behind Dieudonné's conviction.

Finally France gave up, and the French consul in Rio informed the Brazilian Minister of Justice that extradition demands were to be halted. Dieudonné was released from

Brazilian custody and set free in the streets of Rio. After several weeks an official pardon was granted, and he set sail for France. Back in Paris, he remarried his former wife and again took up the trade of cabinetmaker.

In Belem, the French consul was kept quite busy with reports of crimes committed by escaped convicts from Guiana. In October 1929, Governor Siadous in Cayenne began to feel the pressure from Brazilian authorities and the French consul after reports that many escapees had returned to crime in Brazil. Siadous wasn't a great admirer of the bagne nor of the penal administration; he was sensitive to the plight of escaped prisoners — particularly libérés — and the impossibility of rehabilitation in Guiana. In his official function he was, however, obliged to avoid any scandal that would damage France's reputation. In response to the French consul's report, Siadous urged that certain men be returned to Cayenne, "The return to Guiana of some of these men may have an effect on the others who might think twice before committing crimes."

But most fugitives did not head for Brazil. The trade winds blew west so that from St. Laurent, escape by canoe meant following the French coast for nearly 400 miles.

British Guiana could only be a stopping-off point. The English authorities didn't want their colony filled with criminals from French Guiana. They permitted most to stay only a few days and warned them not to return. If a man was caught a second time, the French consul was contacted and the escaper was placed in detention until a boat from French Guiana came for him.

Arrival on the French islands of Martinique and Guadaloupe meant immediate return to the bagne without any kind of extradition. Only escapees who lost their way would land there, and they were quickly taken aboard a Guiana-bound boat.

Of all locations in the Caribbean, Trinidad was the haven for escaped convicts fleeing Guiana. It was known in the bagne that authorities there wouldn't send escapees back to Guiana, but instead permit them to rest for several weeks. In April 1931, Trinidadian officials stated that all convicts who arrived from Guiana would be given supplies to continue their escape.

From that moment on Trinidad was literally swamped with escaping prisoners. Dozens of boats filled with the ragged and starved convicts washed onto Trinidad's shores. At first they were well treated and the Salvation Army in Trinidad aided them. In time the patience of Trinidadians wore thin and those who had aided convicts in the past now began to look upon them as a nuisance. The "season" of escapers to Trinidad began in early May when the seas were calmer. In the early 1930's, cigar-shaped canoes were a common sight on the open waters of the Atlantic.

The number of escapes to Trinidad soon became an embarrassment to the English officials stationed there. Though they still didn't wish to send them back to French Guiana and it had become unclear if they had the legal right to comply with French extradition demands, the increasing numbers of Guiana convicts on Trinidad was becoming an issue.

Although the British officially opposed the penal colony in Guiana, by the beginning of 1934 pressure became too strong for them. In February of that year, Louis Valest, the new director of the penal administration in Guiana, met secretly with Trinidadian officials. Faced with the dilemma of the fugitive problem, Valest came to an understanding with the Trinidadians and vowed that there would be stricter surveillance in the penal colony. New measures to prevent escape would be implemented, since the escaped convicts in the Caribbean and Latin America had begun to compromise France's standing in the Americas.

Though the press reported that the number of escapees in Trinidad fell off after 1934, the opposite seems to be true. In August 1937, with forty escaped convicts already there and more coming every week, the British laid down new regulations to expel — though not to Guiana — those who had made the dash for freedom:

1. From the moment of arrival, suspected escapees from Guiana will be imprisoned.
2. After investigation has determined their nationality, they will be expelled; (a) Nationals of countries other than France will be sent toward their country of origin on ships flying their national flag. (b) French nationals, after proof of nationality has been established, will be sent to France, or as a last resort to Martinique. Under no circumstance will Trinidad return them to Cayenne.
3. Trinidad will assume all costs, though it is hoped that governments concerned will assume their fair share.

From Trinidad, most of the French fugitives headed to Venezuela, which lay less than twenty-five miles from Trinidad's coast across a small but treacherous channel called, 'The Dragon's Mouth.'

For many years, the Venzuelans didn't look closely into the pasts of Frenchmen who came onto Venezuela's shores. The authorities knew quite well where they had come from, but it didn't seem to matter as long as the escapers kept out of trouble. The police left them alone if they found work and kept to themselves. When an oil boom in the 1920s opened up the Venezuelan interior, most of the escaped convicts headed to the American-owned fields at Maracaibo for work. Few questions were asked when a skilled tradesman arrived looking for work.

Juan Vincente Gomez ruled Venezuela with an iron fist for twenty years. As dictator he held absolute power and his policy toward escaped convicts never followed a set pattern. Occasionally he gave in to the requests of the French consul in Caracas and placed several of the escapees in custody to await formal extradition to Guiana, but usually he left the fugitives alone. That is until 1930.

That year army officers opposed to Gomez embarked on a plot to assassinate him and seize power. The plot was discovered before any attempt was made on his life and it was disclosed that an escaped convict by the name of Sassé had been hired to carry out the killing.

Enraged, Gomez ordered all French fugitives in Venezuela rounded up and sent back to Guiana. He put them in detention and contacted the French consul, demanding that a boat be sent from Guiana to take them away. It took the French eighteen months to comply. When the boat arrived, Gomez demanded that the captain pay a high fee for each of the prisoners, under the pretext that their upkeep for a year and a half had been expensive for a small country like Venezuela. The ship's officer responded that it was not in his power to make such a deal, his mission was only to transport the convicts to Guiana. The dispute was not settled, so the boat returned to St. Laurent empty.

Gomez then decided to make use of the men held in detention, over a hundred of them were herded together and put to work on road construction. The highway from Caracas to Ciudad Bolivar was chosen, and the fugitives toiled for six months in Venezuela's densest jungle, working virtually bare-handed.

Henri Bauve had been in Venezuela for several years after escaping from the bagne and recalled what happened.

"I had been working for several years for the Standard Oil Company near Lake Maracaibo, constructing oil-drilling platforms. I was paid twenty-five bolivars a day, but could live well on a single bolivar. The manager, an American called Hadde, had complete confidence in me and I was in charge of a crew of ten workers. Needless to say I never intended to return to Guiana, but when the event in Caracas took place, Mr. Hadde was on vacation in the United States. If he had been there, he would have intervened on my behalf and I wouldn't have been sent back since it was the Americans who made the rules, not the Venezuelans. After sitting in jail in Caracas, I served one year in solitary confinement on St. Joseph for escape."

Fugitives from Guiana were spread throughout the republics of South America, in all walks of life. Some found honest work and made new lives, but most rapidly resorted to crime. White slavery gangs were filled with Guiana convicts who, with contacts back in Europe, were able to "recruit" French women for the expensive brothels of Latin America.

Buenos Aires seems to have been their center, and the fugitives formed a sort of loose organization to aid each other and help the penniless. They also made sure that their "members" stuck to prostitution and kept away from narcotics. The police could be bribed to look the other way when it came to brothels, but not drugs. In 1932, French journalist Paul Darlix went to Argentina to investigate this underworld.

"Two o'clock in the morning in the renowned Gomez Arcade, which along with Callio Correntes form 'Argentina's Montmartre,' the flashing electric lights seems to exchange mysterious signals. An indigo stairway marks the entrance to the underground cabaret *Abdoula*. The place, as its name implies, is a fantasy club. It's the playground where the former tenants from the prison of Cayenne gather in the plumage of high society — in white tuxedos to drown themselves with champagne at forty pesos a bottle in an attempt to forget their heavy pasts. Found here is Rancurelli in the company of Baptiste and Nicois, comrades from the bagne... Another man doesn't keep us waiting. It's Leon from Marseilles, who also several years ago escaped from French Guiana to establish himself first in Caracas and then in Montivideo..."

For a handful of Guiana fugitives, the temptation to return to Europe proved too strong. Armed with forged papers, a few of them embarked by ship across the ocean. The non-French nationals usually had little difficulty in their home countries. Most had been convicted while in the French Foreign Legion and didn't have criminal records to hide from. Back in Spain or Germany, the French would rarely hear of them and would rarely press for extradition of foreign nationals refuged in their own countries.

This was not the case for Frenchmen unwise enough to re-enter France after years of absence. They were on the books as escaped convicts and recognition and capture meant immediate return to French Guiana on the Martiniere. But even at large in France, life was far from free.

They were rarely captured by the police, but rather were denounced by acquaintances and members of their own families. Each time the convict ship sailed, she carried a handful of men returning to Guiana for the second time. A letter received by French journalist Martin Lecoq from a fugitive living in Paris implied that fear of denunciation was in some ways worse than the forest camps of Guiana.

"Escape is nothing against the torture of living in a Paris where I have tried to make myself as small as possible. It has been twenty-two years since my escape! Twenty-two centuries. A child has been born in my freedom. I live. I have married. I go on.

"But with all that my greatest misery is that I am alone, fenced in by myself. My wife knows nothing of my past. My child grows up without the slightest notion that I am a convict. And that is because I am a convict for life. I was sentenced to life at hard labor.

"Sometimes I start to shake when someone stops too long at my stairwell, each time there are voices from the other side of my door. Sometimes I want to turn myself in and be through with it and I know that the honest people I have known in the last twenty years would do nothing to help me if they knew the truth. I also think often of killing myself. I suffer to be free.

"There is never freedom for a fugitive. Even in Paris the bagne continues, perhaps even worse than the bagne in Guiana!"

As rumors and published accounts of escaped prisoners filtered across the Atlantic, Hollywood decided to cash in. It couldn't resist the macabre appeal of Devil's Island, the possible screen portrayal of exiled convicts in the jungle guillotined by savage guards. Reference to the penal colony in film can be seen as early as 1925 when in the original version of the Phantom of the Opera with Lon Chaney, police investigators state that the Phantom was an escaped prisoner from Guiana.

In 1929, Blair Niles' *Condemned to Devil's Island* was adapted for film. Starring Ronald Colman as the romantic thief Michel Oban, *Condemned* portrays the penal colony in a somewhat realistic light. The story-line has Colman sent to work as a houseboy in the bungalow of the villainous Vidal, chief guard of St. Laurent. His wife, played by Ann Harding, soon falls in love with Colman and they plot to escape together back to France. After escaping through the jungle to Paramaribo, Colman is caught on board a Europe-bound ship and sent back to Guiana. As the film ends, Colman and Harding are reunited in Paris when his term is up.

Not an entirely unrealistic story as prisoners did have love affairs with guard's wives; however, they normally ended with the prisoner sent to solitary confinement on some trumped-up charge. Sometimes the prisoner received a bullet in the head, if the husband caught them together.

The most controversial film was released in 1940, after being delayed over a year for political reasons. *Devil's Island* portrays Boris Karloff as Dr. Gaudet, a respected brain surgeon sent to Guiana for treason after having treated a political revolutionary. Upon arrival, Gaudet arouses the hatred of chief guard Colonel Lucien (James Stephenson) and is sentenced to death after leading an unsuccessful rebellion to protest inhuman conditions. In an unrelated accident, Colonel Lucien's daughter is injured and requires immediate brain surgery. Lucien's wife forces her husband to let Gaudet operate on their daughter with the promise that he will not be executed. The operation is a success, but Lucien breaks his word and the guillotine is set up for the execution.

Helped by Madame Lucien, Gaudet escapes with several other prisoners but is captured and scheduled once again to die. Madame Lucien intercedes once again and convinces the governor of Guiana to stay the execution. The governor, moved by her pleas, investigates the affair and arrests Colonel Lucien on charges of corruption and brutality.

As France had announced its intention to close the penal colony under the Popular Front government of Leon Blum as early as 1936, *Devil's Island* was written as a mostly historical story. By 1938, however, it was clear that the French government had changed its mind. When the film previewed in January 1939, the French consul in New York protested, calling it anti-French. France decided to ban all further Warner Brothers films from distribution in France and her colonies and under this pressure, Warner withdrew the film from circulation. Sensitive to reports in the international press about conditions in Guiana, France found this type of film particularly annoying. A year later a drastically cut version of *Devil's Island* was released to mixed reviews. France didn't object this time, as World War II had shifted her priorities elsewhere.

Also in 1940, Clark Gable, Peter Lorre and Joan Crawford starred in *Strange Cargo*, a film adapted from Richard Sale's novel *Not Too Narrow, Not Too Deep*. Gable and several other convicts prepare an escape from Guiana and in the process, Gable meets Crawford, a cabaret singer in a sleazy Guiana nightclub. The film was attacked Legion of Decency, on moral grounds for its overt sexual connotations and was banned by police in Detroit and Providence. In its cut version, the dialogue is still spicy. (Crawford to Gable: "What do you want?" Gable: "Guess!" Crawford: "Why, you crummy convict!").

Strange Cargo received mostly positive reviews, as the all-star cast was commended for their dramatic interpretation. *Film Daily* said, "Here is a good, raw, stark melodrama which holds suspense from the start. Frank Borzage has given it expert directional attention, with Joseph L. Mankiewicz filling the duties of the producer. Clark Gable fills his role admirably, while Ian Hunter has never done better work. The acting is high-grade with Joan Crawford giving her best performance to date. Peter Lorre is M. Pig, and most expressive about it."

The overwhelming success of *Casablanca* prompted Warner Bros. to try similar themes and almost an identical cast in the 1944 release of *Passage to Marseilles*. Adapted from the novel *Men Without A Country* by Charles Nordhoff and James Norman Hall (authors of *Mutiny on the Bounty*), Capt. Freycinet (Claude Rains) tells an English newspaperman about the sordid pasts of a Free French bomber crew. Matrac (Humphrey Bogart) leads Renault (Phillip Dorn), Marius (Peter Lorre), Petit (George Tobias) and Garou (Helmut Dantine) on a Maroni River escape from a St. Laurent lumber camp.

Flashback upon flashback tell of Matrac being framed by French fascists for his opposition to the Munich Pact and sentenced to nine years in Guiana. A chronic rebel often sentenced to solitary confinement on St. Joseph (perhaps Nordhoff and Hall had heard of Roussenq), Matrac cries from the bottom of an excellently re-created reclusion cell, "French justice! Beautiful bunch of rotten fascist flunkies!"

Renault is a sensitive World War I deserter, captured after trying to enlist in the French Foreign Legion in an effort to redeem himself. His shame remains as strong as ever as he watches the French tricolor being raised every morning in Cayenne. His only hope is to escape and join the Free French. Marius, a sleazy but likable thief from Paris, wants to fight for the Free French to see Paris restored as the capital of pleasure and crime.

The convicts escape Guiana in a stolen canoe and are picked up after seventeen days at sea by a tramp steamer. They claim to be gold miners from Venezuela, but they are not believed by the Vichy-leaning Major Duval (Sydney Greenstreet). When news of the the fall of France reaches the Marseilles-bound ship, the captain secretly sets course for England.

Passage to Marseilles did portray conditions in Guiana in an extremely realistic light. The story line, though far-fetched from a convict's point of view, did represent the sentiments of more than a few. Escape to join the Free French was made a capital offence after the Vichy takeover of Guiana, though none were executed for it.

It would again be Humphrey Bogart playing a Guiana convict in the 1955 film *We're No Angels*. Adapted from the play *La Cuisine des Anges* by Albert Huisson, it was translated by Sam and Bella Spewack and made into a Broadway play. Still being produced on stage as late as 1986, it was the first comedy to be written about Guiana convicts.

The 1955 Paramount production had Joseph (Humphrey Bogart), Albert (Aldo Ray) and Jules (Peter Ustinov), as three escaped convicts who break into the store of Felix Ducotel (Leo G. Carroll) in Cayenne. Felix takes them for libérés sent to fix his leaky roof, and his wife, Amelie, (Joan Bennett) and daughter, Isabelle (Gloria Talbott) adopt them as long lost family. The three escaping convicts decide not to murder the family since they agree that "slitting their throats might spoil their Christmas."

The family is menaced by André Trochard (Basil Rathbone), a greedy relative from Paris who owns the store and has come from Paris to inspect the books, which the kindly Ducotel has never been able to balance. Accompanying Trochard is his handsome but selfish nephew Paul (John Baer). Isabelle quickly falls in love with Paul, but the three convicts, touched by the honest Ducotels and revolted by Trochard and his nephew, set out to settle the family's problems. Both Trochard and his nephew are bitten by Albert's pet viper and die before they can change the ownership papers for Trochard's store. A heartbroken Isabelle soon recovers as the three convicts convince the doctor making out the death certificate that Isabelle is the girl of his dreams. Joseph, Albert and Jules find themselves homesick for the bagne and turn themselves in, confident that they can escape any time they want.

After the success of the book *Papillon,* Allied Artists embarked upon a film project that they hoped would be the greatest film of 1973. Of course, *Papillon* had all the elements of a great film. Despite Charrière's historical fabrication, no other Guiana convict wrote a better story and without a doubt *Papillon* was made for the screen. Thirteen million dollars were spent to recreate Guiana prison units in Jamaica — and from this point of view *Papillon* was a success. The march from La Rochelle to the *Martiniere*, the voyage to Guiana, St. Laurent ... they were all well done. A former guard served as technical adviser and was consulted on every last detail of prison life. But despite an accurate setting, the story line has little basis in fact.

In recent years, French filmmakers have made several attempts to document the real Guiana prison dramas. A 1982 telefilm (with Henri Bauve) called *Lettre du bagne* tells of family members searching for an old relative sentenced to Guiana. And picking up on the same theme, Alain Maline's 1987 *Cayenne Palace* (filmed on location in Guiana) stars Richard Berri in a search all through French Guiana to find his father, sentenced thirty years before for the murder of Berri's mother.

PORTRAITS FROM THE ROGUE'S GALLERY

It was freezing in Paris on Thursday, January 14, 1858. By evening a thin sheet of ice had formed on the cobblestones, making passage through the streets hazardous.

Much had changed in French politics during the past decade. After serving as President of France's Second Republic (creating among other things, the Guiana prison colony), Napoleon III led a coup d'état in 1851 and installed himself as head of the new Second Empire. A hero to many in France, he was detested by Italian Republicans after the French occupation of Rome and its preservation of papal power by force.

At 8:30 pm, Emperor Napoleon and Empress Eugénie arrived at the Paris Opera in their official carriage. An announcement had been made of the evening's events and a crowd of several hundred waited outside to catch a glimpse of Napoleon.

Even before their carriage door was opened, three successive explosions ripped through the night. Cries and splintered glass engulfed the crowd. The Emperor and Empress were hurried inside the opera house as chaos outside mounted. When the first bomb exploded under the feet of the Imperial carriage's horse, a kind of snorting mixed with the human cries.

Eight were killed and one hundred and fifty injured by the blasts. Miraculously, Napoleon suffered only a slight scrape on the tip of his nose from a glass fragment and Eugénie had three superficial cuts.

During the night, Paris was turned upside down and security tightened to avoid mass insurrection. An investigation confirmed that three bombs were thrown in the assassination attempt and by morning twenty-seven people had been arrested.

Interrogations quickly reduced this number to four prime suspects. All were Italian. They were led by Romagnol Felice Orsini, thirty-eight, who had been sentenced to life imprisonment in 1844 for his participation in the Romagne uprising. After an amnesty freed him two years later, he was elected to the 1848 Republican Assembly of Rome and fought French troops sent to protect the Pope. After the defeat of Rome, he went to Genoa and then Nice where he prepared an uprising in Central Italy. Arrested and sentenced to death, Orsini escaped before execution and fled to London. An associate and ally of Mazzini, the Italian republican, Orsini was a member of *Jeune Europe*. This was a sinister offshoot of the *Charbonnerie*, an Italian secret society with the goals and secret practices of the Masons, but methods of the modern day Mafia. In London, Orsini recruited fellow Italians Giuseppi Pierri, Antonio Gomez and Charles De Rudio.

Napoleon III was so shocked by the identities of the culprits that he convened a secret counsel, and invoked the highly repressive Security Act of February 19th. Secret and brutal, it granted powers of arrest and exile without trial of Republican political opponents and "other suspects."

The trial began six weeks later on February 25th, in an atmosphere of security hither to unknown in Paris. Nearly every member of the diplomatic corps was present, as well as the highest officials in France. Orsini was defended by the famous French lawyer Jules Favre, and world attention focused on Paris. A press report of the time described the defendants as follows:

"...Orsini is certainly the most worthy of remark. He is of middle stature, rather stout and as full in face as in body. Without being what may be called distinguished, his bearing at all events contrasts with that of his companions and gives him the air of a man of the superior classes. He wore neither beard nor moustache but only whiskers. If he wore a white neckcloth instead of a black one, he would be taken for an advocate...

"De Rudio is of lesser stature than Orsini and his features are as pinched as those of Orsini are full. With the exception of a thin moustache his face was clean shaven. His face might in other times have been well-favored, but his vagrant and wild existence and vice or suffering or both have effaced whatever traces of distinction or regularity it might have originally possessed. His long hair fell upon his shoulders, and was parted in the fashion of of hairdressers, journeymen or apprentices..."

Orsini declared in court that he was prompted by the highest patriotic ideals to liberate his homeland, and that France had betrayed Italy in the most disgusting way. "In 1848, I hoped with all Italy that the end of Austrian domination had arrived. A Constituent Assembly having been convened at Rome, I was elected to form a part of it. There, seeing a French army land, we thought it came as a friend; but when we saw it had come as an enemy, we were painfully astonished."

De Rudio emerges as practically a hired hand in this incident. Though born Carlo Camilius di Rudio to minor Italian nobility, he had lived in East London in abject poverty while scraping by as a private language tutor. His eighteen year-old wife (whom he impregnated when she was fourteen) was illiterate. Pierri met him at a crucial moment. He offered De Rudio 336 francs to follow him to Paris, where he would be told what was required. Once he heard the plan De Rudio had second thoughts, but stayed after being pressured on grounds of his noble background, and of a gentleman keeping his word. Hearing this the President of the Court commented, "You belong to an honorable family, but you were expelled from school for bad conduct, and then from step to step, you became an assassin for 336 francs."

After a two day trial, the jury deliberated for two and a half hours and returned with a guilty verdict for the four — although with extenuating circumstances in the case of Gomez. The judges deliberated for thirty minutes and then returned to pronounce sentence. Gomez was sentenced to life at hard labor; Orsini, Pierri and De Rudio to death by the guillotine.

A death warrant was served for Orsini and Pierri on March 12th, 1858 and they were publicly guillotined two days later in Paris. De Rudio, however, had discreet friends who may have interceded at the right moment. An appeal for mercy reached Eugénie, who was touched on hearing of De Rudio's wife in London. Napoleon III was also moved and commuted De Rudio's death sentence to one of hard labor for life in Guiana.

Although little is known about De Rudio's life in the penal colony, it is a matter of record that he was one of the very few prisoners ever to escape from the Iles du Salut. It is possible that he may have been helped by prison officials who opposed the Second Empire and Napoleon III's tactics. Officials were often sent to Guiana to get them out of France, much like the prisoners whom they guarded. The only hard facts are that he arrived in Cayenne toward the end of 1858 and successfully escaped from one of the Iles du Salut. On December 10th, 1859, De Rudio with ten other convicts stole the guard's boat on Ile Royale, and made it to British Guiana later that month.

In British Guiana he panned for gold without success and finally sailed for London. Hoping to profit from his experiences, he wrote articles and went on the lecture circuit throughout England. But few of his articles sold and his lectures were not well attended. In much the same situation as in 1858 — penniless and in search of adventure — De Rudio set sail for the United States in 1864.

Evan S. Connell in *Son of the Morning Star* relates De Rudio's early military career:

"... He enlisted as a private in the Seventy-ninth Highlanders, this being a unit of New York volunteers; but what he wanted and felt entitled to was a commission. Once again somebody spoke up. He was discharged from the Seventy-ninth in order to accept a lieutenant's commission with the Second United States Colored Troops — a position few whites would accept. In January of 1866 he was mustered out, but by August of '67 he was again in uniform as a regular Army lieutenant. Three weeks later his appointment was cancelled because he failed to pass a medical examination and because the War Department had learned about his activities in Paris."

"Now, our government seldom holds a man's liabilities against him if he may be useful... so it came about that five weeks after declaring De Rudio unfit to wear the uniform of a United States Army officer, the government restored his lieutenancy. On July 14, 1869, he was assigned to Custer's regiment."

Gold had been discovered in the Black Hills of Dakota, and prospectors were streaming to the region. In December of 1875, the Director of Indian Affairs gave the order to

Indian Chiefs in the area to stay within the limits of already set reservations. If by January 31 they hadn't moved, they'd be considered "hostile" and dealt with by military force.

On June 25, 1876, Custer's forces were brought in to "clean up" the area. At noon, divided into three groups, Custer made his big mistake. Indian forces led by Crazy Horse intercepted Custer at Little Bighorn. All of Custer's group were killed in the ferocious battle that would come to be known as Custer's last stand. 261 men in Custer's regiment died; the Indian victory was total. Of course, they had won the battle to lose the war as the Sioux nation rapidly declined after this.

De Rudio, having made narrow escapes before, came through without a scratch. Attached this day to Captain Reno's group, he was two miles from where Custer was attacked. A press report from the *Tribune Extra* of Bismarck (Dakota Territory) on July 6, 1876, gave this account: "De Rudio had a narrow escape, and his escape is attributed to the noise of beavers jumping into the river during the engagement. De Rudio followed them, got out of sight, and after hiding for twelve hours or more finally reached the command in safety."

De Rudio survived for many years after. He retired from the Army and settled in Los Angeles, but few would believe his stories when he told them during his occasional lectures.

That Alfred Dreyfus became the center and symbol of a cause in France toward the turn of the century is quite remarkable. The Dreyfus Affair, in all its controversy and complexity, has always overshadowed Dreyfus himself. The Affair divided France more deeply than anything since the revolution a century before and evoked the deepest passions of that nation as well as its ugliest prejudices. Dreyfus the man wanted nothing more than to be a good officer in the French Army. Throughout humiliation and imprisonment and years of exile he searched for no causes and sang no slogans, but simply maintained his innocence of the espionage conviction that sent him to rot on Devil's Island.

Born to a prosperous Jewish family in 1859, in the Alsatian city of Mulhouse, his father had turned a small family business into one of the most successful textile firms in eastern France. With the proceeds the family was able to provide Alfred with a comfortable apartment while he attended the War College in Paris. After gaining a commission in the French Army, he married and began a promising career in the military.

Humorless, efficient and thorough, his distinction as the only Jew on the General's staff was overshadowed by his competence as an officer. His wife Lucie fit in well as a classic *femme de militaire*. Captain Dreyfus' reputation as an artillery expert grew, and he seemed destined to become one of the rare Jewish generals in the French Army.

The Dreyfus Affair began on the morning of Saturday, October 13th, 1894. Dreyfus was instructed that morning to report to the Chief of Staff in civilian clothes. This was an odd request — to be called in during the weekend, and out of uniform.

He was received in the office of General Boisdeffre by Major Du Paty de Clam. The major explained that the General had been delayed and that he, Dreyfus, was needed to take a letter, Du Paty claiming to have injured his hand. The Major began to dictate and Dreyfus to write.

After several minutes of dictation, Du Paty jumped across the table and grabbed Dreyfus by the collar. "In the name of France I arrest you!" he screamed. "You are accused of the high crime of treason!"

A revolver was placed on the table in front of Dreyfus — the soldier's way out. But Dreyfus, more from shock than anything else, declined suicide and claimed innocence. He was hustled off to a nearby military jail and held incommunicado.

At his trial, the hardest piece of evidence that the army produced was a written *bordereau* (outline) listing five classified military items. This document was allegedly communicated to the Germans by a French officer. Handwriting experts were called in to judge whether Dreyfus was the author of the *bordereau*. The conclusion of the experts was not unanimous as to the authorship of the document. By the end of the trial, Dreyfus' lawyers were confident of acquittal.

In the late afternoon of Saturday, December 22nd, the seven judges of the military tribunal began their deliberations. While in chambers that evening, an extraordinary event took place. Major Du Paty arrived with a packet of documents bearing the handwriting of the Minister of War. These documents had not been seen by Dreyfus' lawyers and were handed over directly to the President of the Court. Du Paty said he would retrieve the documents after they had been examined, and it has been speculated that in the material given to the judges was a strong implication that if Dreyfus was to be found innocent, the judges would find themselves in an extremely bad position with the Minister of War.

Later that evening, the seven judges voted to convict Dreyfus, sentencing him to the maximum penalty allowed — public dishonor and life imprisonment in a fortified place.

The President of France, Jean Caismir-Perrier, though surprised at the outcome, was relieved to see an end to a potentially dangerous episode. "Well it's over," he confided to an assistant. "I shall not conceal from you that a terrible load has been lifted from my mind by the unanimity of the verdict. Certainly they wouldn't convict one of their comrades — even a Jew — unless they were convinced by unquestionable evidence of his guilt."

Dreyfus' degradation took place on the morning of January 5th, 1895, in the courtyard of the War College in Paris. Troops came from all over France to witness the spectacle. Drawn from the Republican Guard was the seven-foot tall Sergeant assigned to the actual task of tearing the medals and braids off of Dreyfus' uniform and breaking Dreyfus' sword over his knee.

"Dreyfus, you are unworthy to bear arms. In the name of the people of France we degrade you." The seven-foot sergeant moved into position and buttons and braids flew in all directions. There was strict silence in the courtyard, and while Dreyfus was being led away, flanked on both sides by his former colleagues, he shouted in a penetrating voice. "I am innocent! I swear that I am innocent! Vive la France!" The assembled crowd, taken aback by his shrill cry, began to insult the little figure in the now-torn military uniform. *"Salaud! Sale juif!* Bastard!" they yelled as he was led away.

Dreyfus arrived in Guiana in March 1895. Devil's Island, which had been used as a leper colony ten years before, was selected as his "fortified place." Convicts from Royale were assigned the task of constructing a stone hut for him on the island. Meanwhile, Dreyfus was kept on Royale in a solitary confinement cell.

Completed in April, the hut measured four square yards and was topped by an iron roof. The guards assigned to surveillance over Dreyfus were not supposed to communicate with him, but this regulation was observed for only a few days and soon they were challenging him to games of chess.

His rations were brought in uncooked and he prepared his meals on a makeshift grill pieced together from remnants of iron bars found in the old leper colony. In the afternoon he paced the island's desolate shore and looked out to the sea and surf.

Soon the climate began to claim his health. Malaria attacks occurred with increasing frequency, prompting a visit from the doctor on Royale who prescribed quinine and condensed milk. The guards gave him extra rations of bread and coffee. They were keenly interested in his survival since guarding Dreyfus alone on Devil's Island was considered a hardship post and they received extra pay.

On June 9th, the director of the penal administration issued the order that Dreyfus wasn't to be let out of his cell when convicts from Royale came to do repair work on Devil's Island. The order was to prevent Dreyfus from having any communication with the outside world. But it was unlikely that any of the Royale convicts would have talked to him anyway, since little comradery would have felt between them. Dreyfus was an army staff officer convicted of treason and a Jew. Traitors, child molesters and rapists have always been despised by convicts in prisons around the world. Guiana was no different, and they also resented his special status and the treatment given him. Many on Royale said that he should have been shot and thrown to the sharks. His confinement to the hut was a prelude to a harsher and more severe regime.

After Dreyfus had been confined on Devil's Island for a year and a half, his brother Mathieu took action to get the case back in the public eye. He convinced an English newspaper to print a fictitious story stating that Alfred had escaped from Devil's Island. Several days later the story was published in French papers and there was renewed interest in Dreyfus. He had been forgotten by the public soon after the degradation. Alarmed, the Minister of Colonies was quite relieved to hear from Cayenne that there was no truth to these rumors.

At about this time, several letters to Dreyfus were intercepted in Paris before expedition to Guiana. In these letters, written in invisible ink, were coded messages. The Minister of Colonies, when informed of this, ordered the Director of the Iles du Salut to confine Dreyfus to his hut twenty-four hours a day. Further, he was to be placed in leg irons at night and two wooden fences were to be constructed around his hut. The guard was doubled and Dreyfus was now subject to severe physical torture.

Of course Dreyfus was not aware of why these measures were taken. On the second day of leg-iron application the Director of the islands came to see Dreyfus of his own volition and told the prisoner that the irons was not a punishment but a "security precaution." For the first time during his stay on Devil's Island, Dreyfus blew up and the Director of the island noted his outburst. "No, things have to be told as they are. This is a measure of hatred from Paris because they can't strike down a family nor smash an innocent man. Neither he nor his family will ever give up because a most shameful miscarriage of justice has been committed."

Moved by Dreyfus' outburst, the Director did an unheard of thing — he filed an official protest to Paris regarding the measures which he had been ordered to apply to the Devil's Island prisoner. As soon as this protest was received by the Minister of Colonies in Paris, the Director was removed and recalled to Paris. The supervision of Dreyfus was now left to a new Director called Deniel who had a reputation for brutality.

Security measures were increased. David L. Lewis, in his book *Prisoners of Honor,* described it like this: "His limbs were immobilized by four U-shaped bars in iron and fitted into wooden blocks at the head and foot of his bed. Dreyfus lay like a mounted insect from sunset till daybreak. The torture was the final physical version of a crucifixion that until then had been largely mental and spiritual."

The new guards were not like the old ones. They strictly observed their orders not to speak with the prisoner. Dreyfus' ration of wine was reduced and the magazines that he had received up till then from France were banned. Now isolated from the rest of the world and confined perpetually in the small hut, he turned to his small library for distraction. It contained the classics of French and English, and he set about translating Shakespeare into French with the aid of a dictionary and a small handbook on grammar. His mail was now scrupulously examined for any trace of coded message or invisible ink.

The Minister of Colonies, concerned that Dreyfus might die in captivity, sent special instructions to Guiana to be carried out in the event of the prisoner's death. Normally he would have been thrown to the sharks like any other convict on the islands. Fearing that complications would result if this were carried out, the Minister of Colonies send the following message to Deniel: "There would always be doubters who would refuse to admit to his death and accuse you of having allowed him to escape. If he dies, embalm him immediately and send his cadaver to France where it can be seen." The Minster also instructed that Dreyfus was to be shot if he made any attempt to escape or any suspicious moves. Director Deniel ordered a mock alert on June 6th, 1897, where the guards took their positions in case any type of vessel approached the island in an attempt to rescue Dreyfus. During the afternoon of the drill, the prisoner sat motionless on his bed while one of the guards stood over him with a loaded pistol pointed at his head.

As can be imagined, Dreyfus' health deteriorated rapidly from this treatment. The doctor from Royale, astounded at what he saw, made a report and ordered Dreyfus moved to larger quarters.

Dreyfus' new hut on the other side of Devil's Island was divided into two chambers and bars overlapped with wire mesh were installed to separate the two sections. After moving there in August, 1897, the minimal privacy that Dreyfus enjoyed in the first hut disappeared. In the outer room, two guards watched his every move. Outside the hut, a watch-tower armed with a Hotchkiss machine gun was manned twenty-four hours a day.

By December, 1897, Dreyfus began to crack. Director Deniel accompanied the Governor of Guiana on an inspection tour late that month and observed that the prisoner was fighting hard to maintain his self control. Dreyfus glared at the two officials, muttering about the way he had been framed and how his family was being harassed. "Somebody wants a scandal," he was reported to have murmured, "he'll have one."

Obviously shaken by this meeting, the Governor nonetheless wrote a report that gave Paris what they wanted to hear. To admit to have been taken by the sincerity of Dreyfus' pleas would not sit well with the Minister of Colonies. The Governor's report on the state of the prisoner implied that Dreyfus was faking insanity and his allusions to suicide were a bluff. The report itself was written in particularly ambiguous language. "For a man who wished for death more than anything else," it read, "he did not forget to take precautions to stay alive." And the Governor added, "While busy appearing mad, he did not lose control of himself easily."

Meanwhile in France, the Dreyfus Affair began to un-ravel. Allegations of conspiracy and forgery concerning the evidence used to convict Dreyfus came to light. The press ran front-page stories of a cover-up by high military officers and the evidence pointed strongly to a Major Esterhazy as the author of the famous *bordereau* used to convict Dreyfus on treason charges. When brought before a court-martial, Esterhazy was acquitted of any wrongdoing.

The trial of Esterhazy divided public sentiment in France to an even greater extent. Doubts lingered and public opinion roused. On January 13th, 1898, George Clemen-ceau's Paris daily *l'Aurore* published Emile Zola's famous *J'accuse*. In it he attacked the army, the press and witnesses at Dreyfus' trial for complicity in a frame-up. Reaction to *J'accuse* was worldwide and the Dreyfus Affair now became an international scandal, compromising the prestige of France. But despite mounting proof of a conspiracy, the article left Zola open to charges of libel and slander and a month later he was tried and convicted on those grounds.

From the upheaval caused by these revelations, Dreyfus' case came up for revision and on September 29th, 1898, the Criminal Chamber of the Court of Cassation opened an investigation into the facts of the Dreyfus case. In June 1899, the Court of Cassation annulled the original court-martial of 1894, making Dreyfus eligible for a new trial.

On Devil's Island, Dreyfus was confined and shackled in his and hut knew nothing of the Affair that had France in an uproar. His only contact with the outside world now was letters from his family that were censored and restricted to family matters. Any mention of his case was blackened out. He had fallen into a severe depression and began to think for the first time that he might die in his hut and be forgotten.

Following the decision in June 1899 for a new trial, a telegram was dispatched to Guiana. It read: "The Court sets aside and annuls the judgement rendered against Alfred Dreyfus by the first court-martial and sends the accused before the Rennes court-martial board."

After four years and two months on Devil's Island, Dreyfus sailed back to France. Later cleared of all charges and restored into the French Army, his case focused world attention on the bagne. The name Devil's Island was now known throughout the world and became confused with the entire penal colony.

For a decade Devil's Island stood uninhabited, the jungle rapidly taking back the neat paths and clearings maintained during Dreyfus' captivity. The cable that linked the island with Royale fell into disrepair and landing on the island became extremely difficult. The small jetty used as a dock by the supply boats during the Dreyfus years began to crumble.

Benjamin Ulmo became the next "resident" of the island in 1908. Like Dreyfus, he was an officer in the French military convicted of treason and, like Dreyfus, a Jew. There the similarities end. While Dreyfus maintained his innocence during his trial, throughout the years of captivity and living to see his name cleared, Ulmo pleaded guilty and admitted his crime.

Ulmo's wealthy father had hoped that his son would enter into the family business upon completion of his studies. But curiosity led Ulmo to choose a career in the French Navy and at the age of twenty, he sailed as an officer to the Far East. Aboard ship, his superiors noted him to be an outstanding officer with a promising future. They were not aware of his on-shore activities in Indochina.

Ulmo's curiosity had led him to the opium dens, and he rapidly developed a taste for the drug. Very available and quite cheap, he was soon smoking forty pipes a day. For the next few years he kept his drug addiction a secret from his superiors, who continued to regard him as a highly competent officer.

On Ulmo's return to France, however, he found opium to be much more expensive. His father upon died leaving him 80,000 francs — at the time a considerable sum. But he quickly spent the entire amount in opium dens.

At about this time, he became involved with Marie-Louise Welsch, known in the press as 'Lison,' the winner of several beauty contests in France. For a time all was well, but soon hideous scenes began, for the salary of a naval officer was not sufficient to keep an expensive beauty like Lison in silk and diamonds. She threatened to leave, accusing Ulmo of wanting to keep her in rags. Every time Ulmo tried to leave her, he was checked by the seductive smile which he could not conceive of living without.

In desperation and hopelessly in debt from opium and Lison, he broke into a secret naval vault in Toulon and procured secret naval codes and other classified documents. Hoping to sell the material to the German Army, he contacted one of Lison's lovers who was a German officer. But the conditions for the exchange were not right, and either in desperation or from opium-induced insanity, he proposed selling the papers back to French officials, allowing them to keep their secrets.

The clumsily thought-out plot backfired and Ulmo was arrested and charged with treason. He begged to be given a revolver with which to commit suicide, but it was refused. Brought before the court-martial, he was sentenced to life imprisonment plus degradation. At the age of twenty-five, he sailed to Guiana. He would never see the beautiful Lison again and, as a prisoner, there was no way that he could procure opium. His life as an officer over; from now on he would be known as Ulmo the traitor.

Arriving in July 1908, he took over the old Dreyfus hut on Devil's Island. Completely alone on the island, he was not forced to work and as a déporté could obtain books and packages from his family in France. During the first several years on the island, he seemed almost happy to the few who came to the island. Away from the drug-filled decadent life he had led in France, he turned to his small library and plunged into the study of mysticism and philosophy. Pacing the shore of Devil's Island, he was at last at peace.

In the solitude of Devil's Island, the infrequent visits of a priest from Cayenne had a profound effect on him. Whether for convenience (as some have thought) or from actual belief, Ulmo converted to Catholicism and was baptized on the rocky coast of Devil's Island. When hearing of his conversion, his Jewish family in France stopped writing to him and considered him to be dead. Now cut off entirely from the outside world, Ulmo plunged himself further into study.

During the First World War, his solitude was broken by the arrival of a handful of political prisoners brought to the island for treason and desertion. As the war continued, Ulmo wrote to the Governor in Cayenne and requested a transfer to the mainland. He had hoped that because of the war, there would be need of someone of his intelligence to work in Cayenne.

His request was refused. His case had caused too much attention in France and now was no time to grant conditional liberty to a man convicted of treason.

Any prisoner convicted for political reasons, regardless of sentence, could, after fifteen years on Devil's Island, be transferred to Cayenne and live there as a libéré. In 1924,

Ulmo took up residence in the church of the priest who had converted him on Devil's Island. For the next six years, with his food and lodging provided, he did little more than read and play the piano and from time to time taking on odd jobs. In 1930, Ulmo obtained a position as an assistant accountant with the Tannon Company. His employer noted his abilities and he advanced rapidly. Soon he was chief accountant.

In Cayenne, where cars were rare at the time, Ulmo drove around in a Renault. For a while he lived with a Creole woman and he was well accepted by the local population. Yet even with his prosperity, his libéré status and the stigma that went with it bothered him. With the help of friends in France and his employer in Cayenne, he was able to obtain a pardon in 1933. Returning to France the next year, Ulmo was shocked by the changes in his country during his twenty-five years in captivity.

Unable to adjust, he soon returned to Cayenne. "What struck me," Ulmo told reporters who had assembled at the dock when he was to board the Guiana-bound ship and return to Cayenne of his free will, "after twenty-six years of being out of touch with civilization, is the stupidity of this humanity which finds itself so superior. You confuse quantity with quality, size with greatness. Even in the material, you have lost your sense of values. I was deeply shocked on returning to Europe by the spiritual depression of the Old World. Humanity had lost all sense of reality."

For the next twenty years, Ulmo was one of the most respected citizens of Cayenne and upon his death in 1957, almost the entire town came out to pay their respects.

The Seznec Affair refuses to die. Sixty years after Guillaume Seznec was sent to French Guiana in chains for a crime of which he always claimed innocence, the drama continues. One of the most celebrated convicts of the bagne, he is still remembered by the last surviving prisoners in French Guiana. Is it important that Seznec's name be cleared thirty years after his death? Denis Le Her-Seznec, grandson of Seznec, thinks so and has struggled for years for a revision of the case.

Seznec always stuck to the same story. On June 24, 1923, Guillaume Seznec and Pierre Quémeneur left Rennes together by car, hoping to arrive in Paris that night. After a series of break-downs, Seznec dropped Quémeneur off at the Havre train station where he caught a train for Paris.

Over sixty years of controversy and bizarre events follow. Quémeneur disappeared! He may have been seen after this and communicated with Seznec and others, but this is clouded in accusations of conspiracy and cover-up. There is one point that has never been disputed: No trace of Quémeneur's body was ever found. It has never been proven beyond doubt that a murder was committed. And it's possible, (though unlikely) that Quémeneur lived long after this.

Why were Seznec and Quémeneur going to Paris? Seznec always claimed they were going to see an American called "Scherdly" or "Cherdy" the next day. It has been established that both Seznec and Quémeneur were involved in trafficking U.S. Army surplus vehicles from World War I, and were acting as middle-men for the resale of these vehicles to the Soviet Union. Despite France's anti-Bolshevik policy at the time, this traffic was so lucrative that many (often with political affiliations to the contrary) were involved. Quémeneur was not only a local businessman, but an elected member of the legislative assembly of Finistére in north-west France. He was linked to Seznec both personally and professionally, and evidence used at Seznec's trial indicates that Seznec owed money to Quémeneur — a motive.

After Quémeneur's family informed the police that he had disappeared, little action was taken. But as the days went by, police began to smell foul play. On June 28th, Seznec was called in as a "witness" and was interrogated in Paris by police inspector Vidal and his twenty-eight-year-old assistant Pierre Bonny.

On one of his first cases, Bonny was convinced of Seznec's guilt. As the years went by — when the Seznec Affair refused to die and French newspapers made accusations that an innocent man was rotting in Guiana — Bonny wasn't as certain. He had been compromised in the Stavisky financial scandal of the late 1920s and saw how evidence that seems certain can be quite the opposite.

On December 27, 1944, the day that Bonny was executed for his role as the head of the French Gestapo during the Nazi Occupation of France, he expressed regret to the prison doctor for "sending an innocent man to the bagne." His son, Jacques Bonny, in his account *Mon père, l'inspecteur Bonny,* was perplexed at why — at this time — when the Seznec Affair must have seemed like ancient history, his father was so preoccupied with the case:

"...At that time, it was interpreted as a move to have his execution delayed. Today, I don't believe that this was true. In any case — and this is certain — my father accepted his death. He knew too much about legal procedures to have thought that a last minute confession to the prison medical officer would have stayed execution. Any confession that might stop execution would have to be made to the District Attorney.

"In reality, I'm convinced that my father finally came to the conclusion that Seznec was innocent years after his conviction, after a personal review of elements in the case..."

In 1944, when Bonny began to feel the weight of evidence against him, but before his imprisonment and trial, his son states that he told him the following:

"...My son, the evidence against me today is very strong. Exactly as it was against Seznec. During the investigation, I was certain that he murdered Quémeneur. It was only years later that I became positive that Seznec was innocent..."

Seznec was arrested and indicted for murdering Quémeneur on the night of June 25-26, largely on evidence from the police report of Vidal and Bonny. His trial was a sensation, with ninety witness depositions cited for the prosecution. And for an alleged crime that took place without witnesses, with no body ever found. An important piece of evidence for the prosecution was a typewriter found in Senzec's home that had been used to write an incriminating contract between Seznec and Quemeneur. Years later, Bonny confessed to having placed the typewriter in Seznec's home by order of his superiors.

Though several people claimed to have seen Quémeneur after the time he was allegedly murdered, only François Le Her testified to that effect. He stated that he'd spent fifteen minutes talking with Quémeneur (whom he knew), over twenty-four hours after the time of death claimed by the prosecution. Le Her, however, had a checkered past. The Mayor of his town testified that he had failed to pass a "morality investigation" required for entrance into the civil service. As well, Le Her often wore war medals that he hadn't received.

Another strong point against Seznec was that the alleged American "Scherdly" or "Cherdy" couldn't be found. The prosecution claimed he didn't exist.

In an Anglo-Saxon court, Seznec might have been acquitted based on Le Her's testimony. But by the Napoleonic code, a French provincial jury of 1923 was able to return the conviction for murder without premeditation against Seznec. French justice doesn't require unanimity from a jury, just a simple majority. Seznec was convicted by one vote.

The prosecution had called for the death penalty, but with Le Her on record, the judges sentenced Seznec to life at hard labor in Guiana.

On April 7, 1926, Seznec, now number 49302, sailed to Guiana on the *Martinière*. Seznec's business was liquidated to cover court costs and his family ruined. His mother died just before his departure for Guiana, and his wife Marie-Jeanne, now without funds, went off to Paris in search of work as a cleaning woman. His children were scattered to orphanages and convents.

Kept in St. Laurent until a first escape attempt to Dutch Guiana failed, Seznec served a term in solitary on St. Joseph and after that was transferred to Ile Royale. In the bagne he continued to claim his innocence. This was considered odd by guards and prisoners alike. Where did he think it would get him to cry about his innocence here? It's been stated that many guards considered him unjustly convicted and treated him differently. Recent revelations point in the opposite direction. In a letter dated April 1934, concerning an escape attempt on Ile Royale (which Seznec was not a part of), a guard states "...It's troubling to find this same Seznec once again in a sleazy affair. He screams about his innocence in the Parisian press and takes the attitude of a victim, not a prisoner, here..."

Like Dreyfus, Seznec wasn't forgotten. His family spear-headed a series of press campaigns calling for revision of his case and a new trial. Several books and numerous articles were written and meetings held. Unlike Dreyfus, they didn't result in any concrete action being taken.

On Ile Royale, Seznec learned of his wife's death in poverty. He also learned of his daughter Jeanne's marriage to Francois Le Her, the only witness in his favor at the trial, now active in the rehabilitation cause.

Despite all the doubt surrounding the case, Seznec wasn't "free" until 1946, when he was pardoned from the rest of his sentence. In July 1947, he returned to France at the age of 69. He was reunited with his daughter and son-in-law after over 20 years in the bagne.

He didn't stay long. The Le Her household was not a happy one; Jeanne and Francois frequently quarreled violently. Seznec packed his bags and went elsewhere. It was a wise move, since on October 3, 1948, the Le Hers had their worst fight.

For some time François Le Her had taunted Jeanne with the threat of sending her father back to prison. Neighbors had heard him scream "killer's daughter" during some of the loudest fights. With his hands around her throat, Jeanne Le Her reached for her revolver and shot her husband to death.

During her trial, the defense effectively brought in neighbors who testified that François Le Her was dangerous and violent. Defended by master trial lawyer Raymond Hubert, Jeanne Le Her was acquitted on July 20, 1949, and fled with her father to Paris.

In another twist to the Seznec Affair, filmmaker André Cayatte seems to have been delayed by French government censures when his proposed film, *L'affaire Seznec,* was rejected. When French President Auriol finally interceded in 1953, other problems came up. Cayatte had hoped that Seznec would play himself in the film, but on the morning of November 15, 1953, Seznec was run over by a van in a hit-and-run accident.

Or perhaps not an accident at all. Witnesses claimed that the van had been parked on the street for hours. In any event, Seznec wasn't killed outright, but died three months later.

Today the Seznec Affair is far from over. French lawyer Denis Langlois has worked for years and made several discoveries that shed new light onto the Affair. "Scherdly" or "Cherdy" did in fact exist and was interviewed before his death in 1966. He wasn't the figment of Seznec's imagination that the prosecution claimed. As well, access to certain files might uncover new evidence. Under French law, judicial archives may not be made public for one hundred years except under exceptional circumstances, a regulation drawn up in part to protect persons (and their descendants) mentioned in criminal investigations. Opening the files has proved difficult in the Seznec Affair.

The Seznec Affair is exceptional and four generations of Seznecs have been traumatized by it. On a visit to French Guiana in December 1987, Denis Le Her-Seznec, returned to Ile Royale to see if the plaque he'd placed the year before was still there. It was and the inscription reads "*A Guillaume Seznec martyr innocent.*" French justice, has yet to recognize this.

On March 4, 1988, French Minister of Justice Albin Chalandon ordered a new official analysis of the handwriting samples used to convict Seznec. Modern handwriting experts have concluded that Seznec wasn't the author of the incriminating sales contract between himself and Quemeneur and the Seznec family hopes for a new trial and judicial rehabilitation.

On the surface, it seemed that Pierre Bougras had it made. A decorated hero in the First World War, he had earned the Legion of Honor before returning to civilian life as the most prominent dermatologist in Marseille and lived with his wife and daughter in the best section of town.

Behind all this, was much trouble. His wife hadn't failed to notice his frequent absences and it was not long before she knew of his affairs with some of the more provocative women in town. The fights between Bougras and his wife escalated, and finally it became too much for her. She filed for divorce and left with the baby.

At this moment, Bougras' decline began. Drinking and gambling took up most of his time and his debts mounted. The decline was evident to his patients who began to look for other doctors, and to his few remaining friends. The more money he needed the less he could make. For a while his bank looked the other way while he signed bad check after bad check, but Bougras knew that the day of reckoning was approaching.

By the middle of March 1925, his medical practice in ruins and hopelessly in debt, one of his last patients came to see him. Jacques Rumebes was a friend of Bougras from the war and he had been coming to see Bougras weekly for some time. Every week he would arrive and receive an injection as part of his medical treatment. On March 14th, Rumebes had 800,000 francs in his possession when he went to see Bougras. This was not astonishing, for he worked as a bank collector and was on his way to deposit the monthly pay for an entire factory.

By the end of May we find Pierre Bougras in jail for non-payment of debts and bad cheques. Jacques Rumebes, who had disappeared in the middle of March, had yet to be connected with Bougras. The police speculated that Rumebes had left town with the money and was somewhere in hiding — not a difficult thing to do with 800,000 francs.

Finally, the police came across a connection between the two men and Bougras was taken from the jail to his medical office. After an extensive search of the examining room, they discovered the partially decomposed body of Jacques Rumebes.

Under police interrogation, Bougras admitted to having been with Rumebes at the time of death. However, during all the interrogations, throughout the long months of detention and during his trial he constantly maintained that he did not murder his friend. Over the months he gave several versions of what had happened, one being that Rumebes, who Bougras claimed had been in great distress, committed suicide in his office. Another version was that Rumebes has a severe allergic reaction to his injection and Bougras hid the body in panic.

Whatever the case may have been, after the long parade of experts and police at his trial, Bougras was convicted of first degree murder. There were doubts after all the contradictions in Bougras' testimony. That, and perhaps the Legion of Honor that Bougras earned during the war, saved his neck from the guillotine and he was sentenced to life at hard labor in Guiana.

Aboard the *Martiniere*, Bougras, convict number 49443, arrived in St. Laurent at the beginning of 1928. He was put in the barracks with the other prisoners and awaited assignment to one of the jungle camps.

But his reputation as a doctor carried with him to the bagne and the head doctor arranged for him to be given a job in the hospital's laboratory. During the few months that he worked there, he was not obliged to sleep with the other convicts in the barracks and soon became friendly with the head prison doctor.

His stay in Guiana was not to be a long one, for on the afternoon of August 30th, 1928, the prison hospital's laboratory was found empty — Bougras was missing. After serving six months of a life sentence he had gotten away.

There was an uproar in the official circles of the bagne. The Bougras case had attracted a great deal of publicity in France the year before, and was still fresh in the minds of the public. His escape would cause heads to roll and the guards to blame the officials for letting him work at the hospital. The officials would blame the higher-ups for not sending enough doctors to the bagne, forcing them to use someone of Bougras' skills in the first place.

While all this was going on, Bougras and two other men passed the Galibi light in broad daylight and entered into the open sea. After twelve days they reached the coast of Venezuela's Irapa region. They were immediately recognized by local police as having escaped from Guiana and thrown in jail. They were to await transport to Caracas where the officials would decide whether or not to hand them over to the French.

At the time of Bougras' arrival in Venezuela, the entire Irapa region was being hit by a severe epidemic. There was no doctor since he had been one of the first to die. The bodies piled up faster than they could be buried. In prison, Bougras was able to convince his jailors that he had been a doctor and was taken from the jail to care for the sick. After several weeks, the epidemic showed signs of letting up and Bougras had saved dozens of lives.

When it was time for Bougras to be sent to Caracas, the natives and police of the region pleaded with the authorities that Bougras not be sent back to French Guiana. The Dictator Gomez got word of the story and after some reflection decided not to send Bougras back to Guiana, despite the emphatic insistence of the French consul in Caracas. While his two companions were returned to St. Laurent, Bougras was permitted to stay in Venezuela as long as he kept quiet about the affair. He was also permitted to resume his practice as a doctor provided he didn't work in Caracas. He would be permitted to visit the city, but not work there. He chose the island of Margarita off the Venezuelan coast and built a small clinic there. He married and had two daughters with his new wife.

Yet Bougras still dreamed of seeing France again. Often when visiting Caracas, he would go to the port of La Guaira and go aboard the French ship to speak his native language and drink with the crew.

Once when aboard a French ship, he was locked in a cabin just before the ship set sail. He was smart enough to contact one of the deck hands who informed the police that he was aboard. The ship was denied permission to leave until Bougras was handed over. It was lucky for him, since return to France would certainly mean a return to Guiana and solitary confinement on St. Joseph.

Bougras never saw France again, though he tried years later to have his case re-opened. He employed a prominent Caracas law firm which tried and failed to get the French to reconsider his case.

Bougras died on Margarita in 1961, where he had lived and worked for over thirty years. He was a hero to the Venezuelans, but still listed as a wanted criminal by the French.

It wasn't his crime that gave him the notoriety he held in the bagne, nor an escape. But through self-inflicted punishments, Paul Roussenq became one of the best known and most feared of the Guiana convicts.

At seventeen, he was arrested for vagrancy and because of his vagabond record was sent to an African disciplinary battalion for military service.

In 1908, Roussenq was locked up in a stone cell for an infraction of the military code. In an attempted suicide, or perhaps just some vague protest against military life, he set fire to his mattress. The fire was soon put out and damages were assessed at five dollars for the mattress.

For destruction of state property and assault, Roussenq was condemned by a military tribunal to twenty years at hard labor. The severity of this sentence may seem astonishing, and even at the time was considered harsh, but in 1908, in the disciplinary battalions of the French Army, one didn't fool around with state property and Roussenq's reputation as a rebel didn't set well with the military judges.

At twenty-two Roussenq sailed to Guiana on the convict ship *Loire*. From his arrival in Guiana, he started a one-man war against the penal administration, the guards and anyone else who gave him the slightest displeasure. His rebellious nature had him insulting and spitting on the officials for slightest real or imaginary affront. This type of behavior sent him to solitary confinement.

This is where his legend lies. Paul Roussenq holds the undisputed record for punishment in the bagne. He endured 3,779 days in the reclusion cells on St. Joseph. Over ten years of his stay was in the five-by-seven foot cells, where even the strongest-willed men have had enough after several months. Much of it was in the 'black hole' cells where no light could penetrate, until the use of these cells stopped in 1926 after the revelations of French journalist Albert Londres.

Paul Roussenq, convict number 37664, became known as "King of the Dark Cells." The solitary confinement guards were instructed not to linger near his cell, for the slightest provocation would have this man screaming at the top of his lungs and the entire solitary confinement block would be in an uproar. The guards knew that this was not a man to play games with.

In the depths of his cell he could be seen pacing. Standing five feet, eight inches tall, yet weighing less than a hundred pounds, his body had been wasted by tropical fevers and the bread and water diet. His glaring eyes frightened even the guards and they preferrred to take little notice of the scraps of paper that made their way into his cell, something strictly forbidden in solitary confinement.

What kept Roussenq in solitary confinement? His file was one of the thickest in Guiana. It weighed several pounds and contained a long list of convictions, infractions and observations that had added time to his stay in the cells. It read like this:

Tearing and destroying prison uniform — thirty days solitary confinement.

Calling out to other prisoners in solitary confinement — thirty days solitary confinement.

Refusing to be put in irons at night — thirty days solitary confinement.

Refusing to be let out of irons in the morning — thirty days solitary confinement.

Accusing a guards of having stolen two francs from him — sixty days solitary confinement.

For putting his head between the bars of his cell and screaming to the guards, "Another punishment if you please!" — thirty days solitary confinement.

It went on like that for dozens of pages and over the years the guards came to the conclusion that the only way to punish Roussenq was not to punish him at all, but every month he had another charge against him. His reputation even reached the office of successive governors of the colony.

And what did he do during most of the time he spent alone in the cells? Flanked by thick stone walls on three sides, with the scribbled graffiti above his cot that read "Roussenq spits on humanity," he embarked on writing an epic poem on life in the penal settlements. Entitled *Hell* it ran over 300 verses and he was still writing it when he was let out of solitary confinement. In addition to this epic, he wrote many letters to officials of the penal administration and to the Governor himself.

When Governor Chanel arrived in Guiana in 1926, one of the first letters he received was from Roussenq. The name meant something to the Governor since he had gotten several letters from Roussenq's mother in France pleading that the new Governor show mercy on her son. She claimed that her son was not beyond hope and deserved a pardon.

Roussenq's letter to the Governor was quite different. "You are like all the others," he wrote. "You are a vampire, an assassin, a degenerate. I'm not afraid of you. I would like to shit on you." It went on like that for four pages, spewing out the vilest of insults, coupled with threats. Nonetheless, Governor Channel had become interested in his case, and when he came to the islands on an inspection tour he told Roussenq that if he watched his step and didn't earn anymore punishments, the Governor would see to it that he receive a pardon.

In 1929, after completing twenty years as a convict, Roussenq became a libéré and moved to St. Laurent. The ten years in solitary had taken its toll on him which is best reflected in a verse of his epic poem:

I am no longer a man
For prison has entered into me
And I am the prison.

In 1932, Roussenq was pardoned from the rest of his doublage and returned to France amidst a mild press campaign. Interest in him quickly died down and he disappeared for some time in the south of France.

During the Second World War he set about to write his memoirs and from it the frightening *l'Enfer du bagne* was published in 1950. Roussenq did not live to see its publication. He committed suicide the year before at the age of sixty-seven.

After serving with distinction in the French Army, René Belbenoit was having a hard time in post-World War I France. Without money or connections, the few jobs open to him paid just enough to permit him to eat. This was not sufficient for a young man who had been through the war and was hoping to marry the young nurse who had treated him in a military hospital. How could he marry her without a good position?

In desperation, Belbenoit turned to theft and after a series of small burglaries was apprehended by the police. Sentenced to eight years at hard labor, Belbenoit sailed for Guiana in 1923.

On arrival, he used all his wits to better his rations and prepare an escape. His first escape from French Guiana took place just a few weeks after his arrival. It lasted several weeks and he was caught not far from Albina in Dutch Guiana.

Punished lightly for this first attempt, he soon proved to be a nuisance to the guards, refusing to work and constantly writing letters of complaint to the officials. He wrote to the governor, the director of the penal administration and to the minister of colonies, complaining about insufficient rations, clothing, etc. He also began to write a manuscript detailing life in the penal colony.

In 1927, American writer Blair Niles and her husband came to visit the penal colony. Belbenoit managed to meet with them and sold part of his manuscript to Niles. Much of his material was used in her novel *Condemned to Devil's Island*, published in 1928, and adapted for film in 1929.

After several more unsuccessful escape attempts and a tour of solitary confinement on St. Joseph, Belbenoit became known to Governor Siadous and was sent to Cayenne to put the colonial archives in order. When Belbenoit became a libéré, the governor granted him a passport with permission to leave the colony for one year. He left for work in Panama, and when the year was up, Belbenoit stowed away on a ship bound for France. He was arrested immediately upon arrival and placed in solitary confinement to await the next sailing of the *Martiniere*. Though granted permission to leave Guiana by the governor, Belbenoit broke the strict regulation against entering France while still a libéré. Returned to Guiana in 1933, he served one year in solitary confinement on St. Joseph.

Belbenoit was made a libéré for the second time in 1934, and a year later escaped from St. Laurent with five others. From Columbia, he made it overland to through Central America and in Nicaragua stowed away on a Los Angeles bound ship. He reached New York by bus at the end of 1936.

In New York, Belbenoit quickly put together a manuscript describing his life in the penal colony. Published in 1938 under the title *Dry Guillotine: Fifteen Years Among The Living Dead*, it was soon on the best-seller list.

The French government watched the case with interest and soon was pressing U.S. authorities for Belbenoit's extradition. He was also jailed by the U.S. Immigration and Naturalization Service for illegal entry into the United States. He was befriended by several prominent personalities — Austin McCormick, corrections commissioner of New York and Richard McGee, warden of Rikers Island prison. A bill was introduced before Congress by Representative Caroline O'Day of New York, to grant Belbenoit permanent residence in the U.S.

Saved from return to Guiana by extension after extension of his visitors permit, Belbenoit married and lectured before law students and penologists. The American Civil Liberties Union began to appeal to the French Ministry of Justice to grant Belbenoit a pardon and, during this time, Belbenoit wrote his sequel to *Dry Guillotine* entitled *Hell on Trial*, and served as historical advisor on the film *Passage to Marseilles*.

Yet by early November 1939, it became apparent that France wasn't going to grant a pardon. In fact, they stepped up their extradition efforts. And the U.S. congress appeared unlikely to act favorably on the O'Day effort for permanent residence. Immigration authorities indicated that Belbenoit had worn out his welcome in the U.S. and granted only a thirty day extension on his visitor's permit. On December 1st, 1939, Belbenoit was given another thirty day extension and told that this one would be his last.

Belbenoit fled to Mexico, but just as quickly re-entered the U.S. by swimming across the Rio Grande. Deported once again, he again slipped across the border, and this time hired an expensive New York law firm. Further extensions were granted to his visitors permit and as World War II broke out, French calls for his return to Guiana faded from war-torn France.

René Belbenoit did eventually become a U.S. citizen in 1956. He settled in Lucerne Valley, California and set about writing a third book called *What Price For Justice*, and made several television appearances. His last book, however, was not finished at the time of his death in 1959, and never saw publication.

———————————◆———————————

There is no doubt that Henri Charrière was a convict in the penal colony of French Guiana. And there is no doubt that he escaped from the bagne during the Second World War. What he describes in his book *Papillon* is largely fictitious in that many of the events and adventures that he attributes to himself were actually performed by other prisoners in the bagne.

Most of the fallacious details in Charrière's two books have been extensively exposed in Gerard de Villier's 1970 account, *Papillon Epinglé*. And the events warrant exposure, since the success of *Papillon* and its sequel *Banco* result from heroics Charrière claimed to have performed and his contention that he was one of the most rebellious and notorious prisoners in Guiana.

Charrière was an unknown. He was a completely insignificant prisoner and gained absolutely no fame during his stay in Guiana. To the handful of former prisoners who knew him, Charrière emerges as a mild and non-rebellious type who did nothing to incur the disfavor of the guards.

Until the publication of *Papillon* in 1968, there was no mention of him at all in any document published on the bagne. And he *would* have been remembered by someone who was there if he had done everything he said he did.

There were famous men in the bagne who arrived in Guiana after having their names and crimes splashed across the newspapers of France. Others gained fame while serving time in Guiana for repeated attempts at escape, or as chronic rebels. Charrière was not one of them. He was one of the thousands of prisoners in the bagne of no particular notoriety.

Charrière was convicted in Paris in 1931, of murder without premeditation of a pimp by the name of Roland Legand. Charrière was also a pimp and not an accepted member of the Parisian underworld as he asserted. He claimed innocence of this crime in *Papillon*, but there is no evidence to support this assertion.

Beginning with his first escape, fact gives way to Charrière's imagination in his description of his escape from the prison hospital in St. Laurent. He claimed to have escaped three weeks after his arrival. In reality, it was a year later and he wasn't a patient under guard awaiting transport to Royale as he claimed. At the time Charrière was employed as an orderly in the hospital and enjoyed a great deal of freedom to wander around St. Laurent. His first escape was in no way remarkable, but his claim of striking one of the guards with an iron pipe during the escape was. The striking of an officer was an extremely serious offense and punishable by death. Charrière served only two years in solitary confinement for this first escape.

It is unlikely that he ever set foot on the leper island that he calls 'Pigeon Island,' located one hundred kilometers from St. Laurent. St. Louis Island, the real leper colony, was much closer to St. Laurent and in no way resembled his description.

The life he claims to have led with the Indians in Colombia during his first escape probably didn't take place then, if ever. It is possible that he lived with them years later, but official records indicate that he was in the custody of Colombian police from the first day of his arrival in that country.

His return to the bagne and his stay in solitary confinement are also exaggerated. Charrière states that during the first two years of solitary he never left his cell. In fact, after 1926, all convicts in reclusion were permitted thirty minutes a day in the exercise yard. His description of discipline on St. Joseph was of a system outlawed years before his arrival.

Charrière also claims to have been in detention with one of the members of the Longueville brothers' escape (though he calls them Grandville). It would be believable, except for one detail. The Longueville brothers' drama took place a decade before.

Papillon claimed to have escaped nine times and toward the middle of his story states that he murdered a fellow prisoner called Bebert Cellier. It is not certain whether a prisoner by this name ever existed — but for this claimed killing Charrière states that he was sentenced to eight years in solitary confinement. This was not possible, since the maximum sentence in reclusion was five years. A few men did serve more than five years in the cells, but they were not sentenced to it. Rather, they incurred the extra time as a result of bad conduct.

Charrière's description of life on Royale is quite fantastic. He gives the impression that the prisoners ran the islands and that the guards had little authority over them. His report of a conversation with a high official on Royale is beyond belief. He says that he promised the director of the islands that he wouldn't escape for six months, the period the director had to serve before retirement. "Sir, I give you my word that I will not try to escape for the remaining time you are here, if it doesn't pass six months," Charrière claims to have said. "I leave in less than five months," was the director's reply.

The idea of making this type of deal with a high official is ridiculous. The discipline on the islands was always very strict, and any convict who spoke like this with an official would soon find himself in the cells.

Charrière's final claimed escape from Devil's Island is a complete fabrication. Very few prisoners ever escaped from the Iles du Salut and none are known to have even attempted escape from Devil's Island, although French records are not clear on this point. It is possible, that he was sent there for a short time. Previously, Devil's Island had been used only for déportés and a transporté like Charrière would never have been sent there for any reason. After the outbreak of World War II, selected transportés were sent there for several months to work. It was not considered punishment, since most requested transfer.

Charrière claims to have escaped from there in 1941 and never again to have returned to Guiana. But there is considerable proof that he spent two more years on the islands. Henri Bauve knew him in Cayenne in 1943, and it wasn't until 1944 that he escaped from the mainland Camp Cascade, not far from Cayenne, in a manner much less heroic than his voyage from Devil's Island on a sack of coconuts. After a pro-De Gaulle regime took over French Guiana in 1943, escape from the mainland camps became relatively easy.

By the time of his death in Spain in 1973, Henri Charrière had made millions from royalties and film rights on his two books. As entertaining as they are, they must be regarded from the point of accuracy as fiction.

THE LIBERATION

After a convict had served his sentence and had survived to see the day of his release, he awaited liberation with a mixture of anxiety and fear.

Fewer than 18,000 of more than 50,000 transportés lived that long. Disease, escape attempts and occasionally the bullets of the guards or the knives of their fellow prisoners had claimed most of them. And the ones who had survived would not be free to return to France, the laws of doublage requiring that prisoners sentenced to less than eight years to reside in Guiana for a period equal to their sentence. Men sentenced to more than eight years would spend the rest of their lives in the colony.

Originally it was hoped that libérés would start farms in the interior and build up the colony, to start families and increase Guiana's population. More than any other plan in the penal colony's conception, this one failed. Libérés, (and relégués given permission to live outside the camp at St. Jean) sank quickly into abject poverty and alcoholism. After years as prisoners, they had neither the means nor the inclination to become colonists. Their liberation in French Guiana was like being in the convict camps, but without the convict ration. Quite a few who had endured years as convicts without falling apart became veritable scarecrows within months after their release.

A former convict known as Pierrot, who lives within a minute's walk of what remains of the St. Laurent prison recalled his "liberation day."

"At eight in the morning I was given a pair of trousers and a wide straw hat. The chief guard handed me a booklet that I was to carry with me at all times, and informed me that I was to report to the police twice a year. I was officially notified that I would have to live within the confines of French Guiana for the rest of my life and that I was prohibited from living in Cayenne for the next twenty years. The gates of the Camp de la Transportation swung open, and I scampered out into the streets of St. Laurent, a free man after ten years. I look around the town, not knowing where I would eat at noon or sleep that night..."

The despair on the faces of the libérés was striking. The hopelessness of the present, the tragedies and mistakes of the past and the bleakness of the future were apparent as they plodded down the dirt streets of Cayenne and St. Laurent. Their bodies and minds broken — but retaining enough energy to hustle for a few francs, the necessary funds for a bottle of tafia, their ticket to oblivion.

In the tattered remnants of prison uniforms or dressed in cut-down flour sacks to clothe their bony nakedness — days, months and years passed, offering nothing but more misery. The men who were not killed within the walls of the prison or in the jungle camps would succumb outside the penitentiary gates for want of a plateful of rice. Most would be dead long before the end of their forced residence, and for those banished to perpetual exile, the lack of any future would soon take its toll.

Near the yellow-brown banks of the Maroni, several minutes walk from the center of town, libéré slums sprang up. This section, known as the Chinese Quarter, boasted some of France's best-known criminals. Without funds, those who had already survived the camps would eke out a living in and around town and return nightly to their hovels, for a tafia-soaked sleep.

An uncommon few were able to better their condition by receiving money from relatives in France. But most had long since cut all ties with their families, if they had any family, out of shame. They were the ones who had disgraced entire villages by their crimes. Their self-respect would not permit them to let their loved ones find out what wrecks they had become.

Cast out by the prison administration, shunned and exploited by most civilians in the colony, one could search the libéré slums and find former libérés, free men — free to return to France on the next boat — but unable to raise the necessary funds for a third-class ticket. The sum needed was not provided by the government and most would never be able to raise it. And even if a libéré could return to France, they normally had nothing to return to. Most of their families had considered them dead for years and after a generation in French Guiana they would most likely end up on the streets and die from exposure in their first winter in twenty years.

The requirements of French Guiana's labor force never matched the number of libérés in the colony. The monthly freighters from France needed manpower for the day or two they were in port to unload cargo. Construction jobs were sometimes available, but libérés were ill-fed and badly dressed and would rarely get these jobs if healthy Creoles applied. One local farmer in the St. Laurent area considered libérés to be bad workers when they did find work: "They aren't steady and leave the fields when they wish without informing their foreman." As for starting their own farms, very few could afford the tools and seed needed to scratch away at the jungle's soil.

In 1930, Governor Siadous addressed the problem of employment competition between convicts under sentence and libérés, as the prison administration hired out convicts to local contractors for less than the existence wages asked by libérés. A gradual reduction of convict labor implemented in that year showed positive results for libérés, but Siadous' term as governor expired and the next administration reversed this move.

Some libérés went butterfly hunting in the jungle — it was often the only way to earn a few francs. It required tremendous patience to catch them, since the valuable ones were not common and usually flew over the heads and nets of the chasers. Perfect specimens could always be sold to traders in St. Laurent and Cayenne who in turn sold them abroad to collectors at five times the price. But it was dangerous, for more than one butterfly chaser had been murdered for his catch by other starving libérés.

No matter how destitute, the Saturday night film at St. Laurent's movie house was the one event never missed by St. Laurent's libérés. Perhaps they were drawn there since it was their only link with the outside world. Seated in the cheapest seats, as soon as the lights dimmed, bottles of tafia emerged from inside their shirts. As the film progressed, and the level in their bottles decreased, their depression increased.

Drunken and hopeless by the film's end, they headed for the libéré village. A few who had saved a little tafia and some money would head to the Creole shacks where the doudous would be waiting. Wracked with venereal disease and looking nothing like the tightly dressed and immaculately coiffed film stars they had seem earlier, these women nonetheless served the purpose.

Though forbidden to leave the confines of the colony, many libérés ventured to Albina at night and engaged in a little small-time smuggling. The Dutch police on the other side, who always sent French convicts back to St. Laurent, looked the other way to this illicit commerce. Libérés caught in Albina were treated less severely than convicts in the process of escape. The Dutch knew that if handed over to the French police on the other side of the Maroni, the libérés faced up to two years in prison.

As a libéré, Raymond Vaudé was caught within Dutch territory during an escape. The police chief in Albina who interrogated him, treated him with some degree of sympathy:

"'You're an escapee, aren't you?'

"The voice that asked me in a very pure English was soft, if not compassionate. He questioned me frankly.

"'Convict?'

"'No, libéré.'

"'What was your crime?'

"I told him truthfully, without hiding anything, and when I was finished he responded with the same frankness, saying that he had no reason to doubt what I had told him. He told me that I must leave Dutch territory immediately, but to save me from punishment he would let me return to St. Laurent without reporting me to the French police.

"'Find a boatman and leave tonight. Do you have any money?'

"I told him that I had but a few francs. With that, he reached into his pocket and handed me several bank notes."

It was not unheard of for a libéré to purposely commit a small crime, just to get caught and be sent back to prison where he would have to be clothed and fed. Even without trying, a libéré might find himself back in the cells or still worse, re-classified as a relégué and banished to the camp at St. Jean. Four convictions for vagrancy were all that was needed, and conditions at St. Jean were in many respects worse than in the convict camps. As well, there was proof that libérés helped convicts under sentence to escape. On May 23, 1935, with libéré crime on the increase, Governor Lamy decreed that libérés may not circulate in the streets at night.

At the time of their release, most convicts were in St. Laurent. After a few weeks of fighting in the public market over a few scraps of rotten fruit with other libérés, those who had had enough made their way to Cayenne. This was no small feat. The 250 kilometers separating the two towns was dense jungle and swamp. If a man didn't have the funds to take the coastal boat (and most libérés didn't) he went overland. No roads had been built to link the two towns and all that existed was a small footpath through the forest. The small creeks had to be waded through and the rivers crossed by raft. The journey often took a week, sometimes longer. But the man who had made the journey in hope of finding something better than the misery of St. Laurent was in for a surprise.

The doublage originally meant total freedom within the confines of the colony, but as the libéré presence became too much for the inhabitants of Cayenne, successive governors tried to limit their number in the capital. As of 1906, Cayenne was officially made off-limits to libérés and a demarcation point twelve kilometers from the center of town was the boundary. But this restriction was an administrative move, drawn up to keep undesirables — libérés who had fallen out with the administration — at arms length. In reality, dozens of libérés lived clandestinely in Cayenne and hundreds lived there legally, since the residence restriction could be lifted in cases of good conduct.

Some libérés were given permission to come to Cayenne on Thursdays and Sundays during daylight hours, but were liable to arrest at other times. This was to permit libéré farmers outside town an opportunity to market their produce and purchase supplies.

Cayenne had never been much – a few dirt streets with government offices and Chinese stores mixed in with the wooden homes of the more prosperous civilians. The only place of interest was the Place des Palmistes, a park in the center of town flanked with hundreds of Traveller palms. Ever-present ragged libérés wandered around aimlessly, rolling cigarettes from butts found in the street. The outskirts of Cayenne were a center for vice. Stills slapped together from old gasoline drums distilled rum from the sugar cane growing nearby, the rawest tafia from these stills being sold in the cheaper Chinese stores and in the slums of Cayenne.

The usual slavery was reversed in Cayenne as the whites served the blacks. Penniless libérés were seen daily at the public market shopping for negro employers. White convicts and libérés cleaned the streets and emptied latrines; poor Creole farmers employed white servants and low-grade colonial officials often had several. They were paid pennies a day.

A black woodworker from Surinam was startled upon his arrival by boat in Cayenne: "When I first landed at the port, several white men scrambled to carry my bags. This had never happened to me before."

A small number of talented libérés found jobs as butlers and cooks to high officials and civilians from France. Convicted murderers seemed to have the best chance at these positions — they were considered more reliable than thieves and rapists. For the majority of libérés, however, there was no work, since convicts under sentence could be hired out for even less money.

Out of work, former convicts congregated in the town's slum district called 'The Creek,' since it was separated from the rest of Cayenne by a small canal. Filthy and living in abject poverty, residents of this area survived by maintaining small plots of land on the outskirts of town.

The open sewers in this section were often clogged from the rains and the stench that wafted from an accumulation of sewage, drowned rats and garbage was revolting — though most of the Creek's residents, long used to this filth, did little to improve things. The native whores who lived there, as in St. Laurent, would accept payment in tafia as well as cash. At siesta time they could be seen peering out of their shacks beckoning to customers while the vultures swooped down, scavenging the garbage-littered streets. At night they sold their diseased bodies less discreetly by standing in front of their shacks, the vultures now replaced by fluttering bats.

Cayenne would win no prizes for virtue during the prison era. The town had electricity only at certain hours and running water just two hours a day. Without convicts and libérés, Cayenne would perish for want of manpower, and with them, the accumulated vice and corruption made Cayenne's residents into a decadent, incestuous lot.

The number of development plans proposed by governors and officials couldn't be counted. Rubber would be tried for several years, then cattle, then back to rubber — all to satisfy higher officials in Paris that something was being done to build up the colony. None of the development plans amounted to anything.

The Creole population took little notice of these bureaucratic moves. At the first opportunity they left the fields and moved to Cayenne in hopes of finding desk jobs with the government. They considered heavy labor degrading since several generations had grown up seeing convicts herded together under guard, and until 1926, chained. New development plans would be implemented just as soon as the old ones failed. The politicians would get their cut and the importers would profit. The colony continued to grow more and more dependent on subsidies from Paris and the interior remained virgin and unexplored jungle.

Though many governors tried to improve living conditions for ex-convicts, the only organization to put plans put into effect was the Salvation Army. Headed by Major

Charles Pean, a hostel outside the restricted area of Cayenne in Montjoly became the refuge for libérés who had no other place to go. They were assured of a roof over their heads and three meals a day. In return, they were set to work in farms that had been created by the Salvation Army. The money earned by libérés was put aside for a return ticket to France for those sentenced to less than eight years.

Far from being grateful, the libérés cursed Pean behind his back and stole everything that wasn't bolted down.

But Pean understood the men he had come to help. He realized that life in Montjoly wasn't much different from being in the prison camps. No one forced the libérés to stay there, so to voluntarily go back to communal life with other ex-convicts was a severe blow to their pride. Men who would have to remain in French Guiana for the rest of their lives took it the hardest since Montjoly was the end of the line for them. For a man of thirty-five with no hope of ever returning to France, three meals a day and a cot was little in the way of compensation.

And the libérés really did have little to be grateful for. Though Pean couldn't be described as a religious fanatic, and was never known to cajole the men into prayer, some of the other Salvation Army workers did. Pean's manner must have appeared to be a tactic, a tactic to get them to convert. It would seem ridiculous to an ex-convict who had spent years in the bagne that Charles Pean of the Salvation Army was in French Guiana to help them only from the goodness of his heart.

Libérés were also prohibited from re-entering France and could only leave the colony for a third country with special permission from the governor. In practice it was rarely granted, since a libéré who left Guiana would be extremely reluctant to return at the expiration of his limited passport. Only the rare libéré who had prospered in the colony and needed to go to neighboring South American countries on business ever applied — and permission was not always granted, even to these men. It was out of the question for the penniless wrecks living in the streets. Also, few consuls of foreign countries were represented in Cayenne and those who could grant visas would almost always reject the application of a libéré.

For the most part, the civilians of French Guiana were apathetic in the face of French colonial rule and the colony's use as a dumping ground for French criminals. But in 1928, Cayenne's normally docile populace erupted into violence over the mysterious death of Jean Galmot. For several days the town was in a state of anarchy, and law and order was only restored when the governor called in troops from Martinique.

Who was Jean Galmot? He was a Frenchman whose fascination with French Guiana began early, as he watched his country being ripped apart by the Dreyfus Affair. Upon leaving school, he worked for a time as a freelance journalist and on the staff of several small French newspapers.

Marriage to the daughter of a wealthy American diplomat was at first happy but after several years, their extravagant life-style left him with many debts. His father-in-law, hoping to instill in him some measure of responsibility, sent him to Guiana where he had an interest in a small and not very prosperous gold mine on the Mana river. Galmot arrived in French Guiana for the first time in 1906.

The gold mine didn't interest him, but he became fascinated with the plant and animal life in the jungle. After six months he returned to France and convinced several French firms to loan him money to export tropical wood and rum. He became active in local politics, attracting a large following among the creoles. When he left for France in 1915 he was the most popular figure in the colony, known among the Guianese as "Papa Galmot."

The First World War proved to be a great opportunity for him, since the military lacked rum and he was one of the few suppliers. Galmot made a fortune as he was able gain exclusive control over the export market from Guiana and the French West Indies.

In 1919, Galmot was back in Cayenne and running for elective office as deputé of French Guiana. His charm and his reputation as a businessman led him to a landslide victory. Expanding his business activities, he began to pose a threat to the old established French firms with whom he was in direct competition. His enemies were influential, and in 1923 they banded together to destroy him. Galmot was charged with fraud and later that year convicted by a Paris court. He was sentenced to twelve months in prison, his business collapsed and Guiana was without a deputé. In 1924 his seat as deputé was being sought by Eugene Lautier, a newly arrived Frenchman who had failed to get elected in any district in France.

His prison sentence complete, Galmot hurried back to Guiana in time for the election. His popularity among the Creoles had, if anything, grown during his absence since they all believed that his trial and conviction were a frame-up, arranged to destroy his ambition of declaring French Guiana an independent state. Papa Galmot became a symbol as the white Frenchman who would lead the Creoles to liberation and out of colonial repression.

Galmot lost the 1924 election. There were cries of electoral fraud as Lautier was installed as deputé with a 200 - vote plurality. Nearly all of Cayenne had voted for Galmot and fighting erupted in the streets. The governor and mayor, both Galmot opponents, called out the troops to restore order.

Between 1924 and 1928 French Guiana was rocked by scandal after scandal. The government was accused of taking kick-backs for granting mining concessions in the interior. In 1928, Galmot again challenged Lautier and was again defeated under the same fraudulent conditions as in 1924.

For the Creoles this second defeat of Papa Galmot was too much. A large crowd armed with machetes and rifles gathered in front of the Governor's House and demanded a recount. Lautier and other Galmot opponents, fearing attack, hid in the Bank of Guiana's vault.

An official recount later proved that Lautier had received 2,000 votes from residents long dead or no longer in the colony. Galmot was declared the winner. His supporters were jubilant and his enemies planned revenge.

On Sunday August 5, 1928, Galmot — who suffered from chronic malaria — was burning with fever. This was no normal attack, since he was unable to swallow and he seemed in great pain. A doctor was called in and immediately brought him to the hospital — but it was too late. He died several hours later, and the doctor tentatively concluded that arsenic poisoning was the cause of death.

Infuriated by the murder, Cayenne erupted into riot. Nine Galmot opponents were rounded up and executed in the Place des Palmistes; dozens more were injured. The governor fled to the Isles du Salut for safety, while the head of the Bank of Guiana, dressed as a convict, took refuge in the Cayenne jail. The rioting and looting lasted for days and in the confusion, libérés carted off as much as they could carry.

Galmot's life and death attracted the interest of writers of the era. In 1930 Blaise Cendrars published *Rhum*, a biography of Galmot and also in that year the American novelist Blair Niles chose Cayenne at the time of Galmot's murder as the setting for her novel *Free*.

THE END OF A HELL

As soon as France began to use French Guiana as a penal colony, there were pleas for its abolition. The opposition began as far back as 1852, the first year of transportation to Guiana. On Sept 28th of that year, the *Report From the Colonies* stated:

"French Guiana has acquired a special importance since our government has made it a penitentiary colony. Already several thousand prisoners have been transported there along with men condemned for political reasons, who ought not be confounded with assassins and highways robbers. What will be the result of this experiment? Will the penitentiary colony succeed? Many competent judges think not. The climate is fatal for Europeans and the country is covered with forests and marshes exhaling a pestilential vapor. Poor political exiles. Are they condemned to perish in this remote land?"

And so for the next ninety years opponents of the bagne made their repulsion known, while proponents voted funds and watched approvingly as the twice-yearly convoys made their way to Guiana. In France, Cayenne took on the reputation of a center for thieves and assassins, where men toiled in the jungle and never came back.

The high mortality rate, coupled with the bad reputation of Guiana's climate, prompted the French government to suspend the convoys to Guiana in favor of New Caledonia where the climate was milder and the need for manpower greater at the time. It lasted for fifteen years, but the New Caledonia experiment fell out of favor as a result of scandals and the enormous cost of transport.

The penal settlements became known to the world at the time of the Dreyfus Affair, but the scandal didn't produce an international outcry against the Guiana prisons. After his return to France in 1899, Dreyfus was never known to have voiced opposition to the penal colony, and many have concluded that he considered Guiana to be a just punishment for espionage.

Before the World War I, there were conflicting reports about Guiana in the popular press. The war halted convoys to Guiana; a generation later, the penal colony would be of little interest with Europe again in turmoil.

The convict convoys resumed in 1921, but events in the post-war era made them less than regular. The first press campaign to abolish the bagne began in 1923 with the revelations of French journalist Albert Londres. His reports spurred other investigators to go to Guiana, and most returned to publish gripping, though often exaggerated, accounts in the French press. But the controversy produced results.

In November 1924, an international commission was set up to investigate charges brought about in the press. They rejected the idea of abolishing the penal colony, concluding that new prison construction would be too expensive. They did recommend that conditions in Guiana warranted improvement, even though they were better in many aspects to prisons in France.

Among the commission's recommendations was that solitary confinement with enforced silence be abolished, and that libérés be aided so they didn't fall into alcoholism and poverty. The commission felt that through these small reforms the bagne could continue; if not a paradise at least as an establishment that would not besmirch the honor of France in the western hemisphere. It was felt that through small reforms the "problem of the bagne" could be solved.

But these points were not well understood to those who read them in Paris. The official visits to Guiana were very selective; they lasted just forty-eight hours and the delegation was shown very little of the penal colony by Cayenne officials. The bagne had become quite lucrative for those who ran it and the minor colonial officials didn't want it closed. Their careers were solidly linked with the penal colony's continuation, and any investigation with the possible aim of abolition was very threatening to these colonial officials.

Also, the 1926 commission was strongly influenced by political pressure in France. French President Gaston Doumergue was at the time unwilling to address in detail the problems in France's smallest and most remote colony. He had stated that not until France had made progress in her more pressing domestic and international problems could the Guiana prisons be fully reformed.

Yet all this came at a time when the Ministry of Justice reported in a study that the bagne was a failure in all that its creation set out to accomplish. "As a method of colonization," the report stated, "transportation has produced negative results. The law of 1854 has failed completely from a double point of view, that of the expiation of crime and the improvement of the condition of the convict. The most varied types of discipline have been tried and all have failed — humanitarianism no less than brutal repression.

"The moral failure of this system is even more lamentable than its economic failure. Not only is the correction or improvement of the occasional criminal rendered impossible, but each individual is contaminated morally and physically by the hideous conditions prevailing around him."

There had already been one sailing of the *Martiniere* in 1926, the first in two years. Later that year, a second convoy was readied for transport to Guiana with the announcement that this would be the last. When this convoy sailed, another was readied and during the 1920s, each convoy destined for Guiana was officially designated as the last. In fact, the largest convoys to Guiana — often with more than 700 convicts — sailed during this era.

The controversy continued, as many opposed the penal colony on moral and legal grounds. Increasingly, pressure was brought forth to close the bagne for more diverse, even bizarre reasons. In March 1926 a prominent French scientist rejected the original plan to have ex-prisoners marry Creole women to encourage population of the colony. He stated, "Nothing can come of such a union except a race of super criminals."

Others wanted to change the location of the bagne on account of the climate, thought of as unhealthy for Europeans. Maurice Archambault of the French Chamber of Deputies proposed that the penal colony be transferred to the Kerguelan Islands near the Arctic Circle. He stated that though the winter was very long, the summer months provided an excellent opportunity for the convicts to raise crops since the soil was very fertile. This was the first proposal to transfer the "green hell" of French Guiana into a frozen Siberia-type hell.

Movement toward the closing of the penal colony intensified during the 1930s. Convicts awaiting transport to Guiana in La Rochelle rioted when the *Martiniere* was three months overdue in December 1929. Some had waited over a year and the strict discipline caused many to lose patience.

The Latin American Press hadn't ignored the penal colony either. Most South American countries had long been reluctant "hosts" of escaped prisoners and in January

1932, an editorial in the Colombian newspaper *El Tiempo de Barranquilla* launched a scathing attack on the penal colony entitled *Shame for the Americas.*

"France gains nothing from this penal institution. Every year she loses millions. She loses most of all prestige as a colonial and humanitarian nation. This penal colony is a disaster which dishonors both France and the Americas. French Guiana is a horrible cancer which requires urgent surgical intervention for the sake of international hygiene and for the honor of the Americas, which have been soiled by this survival of slavery in its most intolerable form — state slavery."

In July of 1929, sensitive to press reports that detailed and often misled the public, Governor Siadous banned all visits to the penal colony without the written consent of the governor. Photos were prohibited and regulations enforced. When, in June 1934, a Pan American plane flew over Camp Kourou twice in order to let passengers photograph convicts at work, the governor warned that a second incident of this type would result in seizure of the aircraft.

In 1933, voices from France again began to call for the suspension of transportation. In July of that year, reports began to circulate that movements to suppress the convict settlements had arisen in legal and parliamentary circles of the French Government. Of course, so many other reports had circulated over the years that this one couldn't be given all that much credibility. But the debate had begun. The argument against abolition of the bagne was headed by Deputé Maurice Garcon. He concluded that if there was no longer an overseas penal settlement to deter criminals, courts would be forced to pass more death sentences. They could spare the lives of murderers if the courts were safe in the knowledge that convicts would be banished to a location very far from France. Garcon argued that further reforms were needed in Guiana, but the concept of transportation was sound.

Deputé Gaston Monnerville was one of the loudest voices in favor of abolishing the penal colony. This young French Guianese lawyer (later to become President of the French Senate) had been elected as the colony's representative after the 1928 fiasco and the death of Galmot. In 1936 he responded to Garcon and proponents of the bagne in the French National Assembly.

"What would be your reaction," Monnerville asked, "if one fine morning while opening your windows you discovered a band of thugs installed on your front yard? You would — and no one would blame you for it — protest energetically against this intrusion. Very well! This is the situation that Guiana has been subjected to for the last two-thirds of a century, thoughtlessly surrendered into incompetence by an administration that has no idea of the extent of the damage it has caused. Our richest colony has become a sewer. Do what you want with your convicts, but don't send them to us."

Monnerville agreed that the penal colony had become an issue much larger than that of domestic penal reform. Citing the bad press, particularly from Colombia, he argued what proponents of the bagne refused to recognize — namely that the penal colony's presence in Guiana had become an international issue.

On a wave of humanitarian reform, the Popular Front government of Leon Blum pushed further for abolition. In December 1936, a commission headed by French Appeals Court President Paul Matter was set up to study legislative proposals concerned with suspending transportation. Its members included Monnerville, Minister of Colonies Marius Moutet and Minister of Justice Marc Roucart.

Of the commission members, Monnerville proved to be the most emphatic. He begged not only for the convoys to Guiana to be suspended, but for the camps in Guiana to be dismantled and all convicts, libérés and relégués sent elsewhere. His pleas were not to be enacted into law, as the Popular Front disbanded as quickly as it was formed and opposition to abolition began to gain force in the French Senate.

To circumvent debate and delay, the legislation was presented to French President Lebrun after it had been approved by Premier Daladier, who had been given decree power just before the outbreak of World War II Daladier included this report:

"For many years, despite improvement of living conditions for transported convicts, there has been severe criticism of the bagne in Guiana. It has in effect not served at all as a criminal deterrent and has provided no means whatsoever for moral reform and rehabilitation. From another point of view, the use of Guiana — the only mainland French possession in the Western Hemisphere — is extremely bad for France's prestige in South, as well as North America. Escaped convicts are scattered throughout Brazil, Venezuela and Colombia where they form dangerous and disreputable gangs. From their presence, suspicion now surrounds all Frenchmen in these countries. Such a situation can go on no longer without having an impact on the prestige of France.

"To have any moral value, penal servitude must subject the convicted to work on a regular basis. Experience shows that convict labor cannot serve as a colonizing force given Guiana's climate. It would therefore seem doubtful to anticipate any betterment of the convicts themselves by their work in the penal colony..."

The decree, signed into law on June 17, 1938, read as follows:

ARTICLE I. Sentences of hard labor are now to be served in metropolitan prisons where the convicts will be subject to cell isolation and a regular work program.

ARTICLE II. The above article is not applicable to convicts already sentenced to hard labor, but not as yet transported by the enactment date of this decree. Convicts already transported will continue to be subject to the law of May 30, 1854.

ARTICLE III. For all convicts serving sentences, whether transported or not by the enactment date of this decree, the temporary residence obligation as specified by Article-6 of the law of May 30, 1854 is replaced by a residence prohibition for twenty years.

ARTICLE IV. The transported libérés actually obliged to reside in the colony will come under the residence prohibition for a period equal to that of the residence obligation yet to run, and in the case of residence for life, to a residence prohibition for a period of twenty years from the expiration of sentence.

The decree was a compromise. Few in France wanted to deal with the 3,300 transportés, 1,800 libérés, and 2,000 relégués in Guiana at the time of the decree. Bringing them home, as Monnerville, had desired would cause immediate need to build new prisons in France.

The decree had the effect of freeing libérés in the colony from their obligation to reside in Guiana. The new residence restriction prohibited them from living in specific areas of France, usually the department where their crimes had been committed. In any case, there would be no mass influx of libérés back to France. They would still have to find the means to pay their passage, and each mail boat had room only for several dozen passengers. It would take years.

And the decree said nothing about relégués. There had been no convict convoy to Guiana since 1935, but soon after the decree had been signed, an announcement was made to a startled France that two more convoys were being readied to sail to Guiana, one for November and a second for the end of 1939.

On November 22, 1938 a recommissioned *Martiniere* (it had been sold to another company) sailed to Guiana with 660 relégués. This would be the last convoy, as the next one was never assembled. France was at war once again.

Events in Europe were far removed from the life and thoughts of those in French Guiana. At the outbreak of World War II, most there had lost touch with France. Only the few guards who had recently arrived in the colony were aware of the magnitude and ambitions of the Third Reich.

So France was at war. What could be thought of that! In the festering tropical outpost of Guiana, who was sleeping with whose wife was a much closer reality. There were infrequent reports from Paris of the fighting, but life went on as usual in the equatorial heat and rain. For the penal administration and guards, lining pockets was important, not politics. It had been stated in official reports that "all too often, accounting practices of the prison administration can't be taken seriously." For the most part, they were in favor of any regime that would permit them to graft, eat and fornicate.

The fall of France in 1940 would soon make this impossible. Rapidly, communication with Europe faded and the stark horror began to sink in that for once they could not look to Paris for a solution. That's how the colony had functioned: follow orders from Paris, and no one will blame you. Apprehension set in at every level of the penal and colonial administration as French Guiana was suddenly cut off from the rest of the world. Food supplies from France were running out. There was confusion. Who was in charge? Where would the money come from to keep the place going? Instinctively the officials looked to Paris, but Paris had ceased to exist and Vichy had enough trouble of its own without concerning itself too heavily with French Guiana.

When Vichy started sending officials to the colony in 1941, most in French Guiana scrambled to declare themselves for Petain. It was difficult for this attitude to spread very far among the Creole population though since Vichy, being an instrument of Germany, could not escape its blatant racist association.

The career prison officials tried to stay out the way of these new Petanistes. Regardless of their own political persuasions, these were not of the same mold as these new officials. During normal times the aims of French colonization couldn't be taken that seriously in Guiana. Being 5,000 miles from France guarding in a penal colony wasn't what was meant by those who wanted to spread French civilization.

But these weren't normal times. It soon became apparent that many of these new officials were downright fanatics. Their effect on prisoners was devastating. The usual quotas of work were doubled while at the same time food and clothing were reduced. The relégués at St. Jean were hardest hit and the death rate rose rapidly to forty percent. Men who had adapted to jungle conditions over the years now gave up, fell and didn't recover.

The Atlantic Blockade cut Guiana off, and there were few places left to turn. Brazil might have been able to supply Guiana, but the administration had nothing to pay them with. Europe was chaos, France had fallen and Cayenne was forgotten.

The career guards were not unsympathetic to the plight of convicts during this time. They too were feeling the pressure. Who knew which Vichy official would find reason to put them in jail? When an escape took place they now felt inclined to look the other way.

Claude Chandon was an active supporter of De Gaulle from the outbreak of the war. He was a veteran of the First World War who had gone to Guiana in 1930 to start a plantation. Just after the fall of France, he approached Robert Chot, then governor in Cayenne, and requested that he be permitted to recruit the Senegalese regiment in the colony to go and join the Free French Forces. His request was refused, the governor citing his orders to keep the regiment in the colony.

When Chot was replaced by an even more ardent Vichy official, Chandon changed his tactics. He now went to libéré slums around St. Laurent and recruited some of the derelicts there to escape with him to Albina and join the Free French.

That men from the libéré slums followed Chandon was not surprising, though their reasons could hardly be considered patriotic. Chandon represented a way out of Guiana and its misery. De Gaulle, Petain and Hitler were just names from a country which had made them outcasts.

In February 1941, sixty libérés followed by an equal number of relégués crossed the Maroni into the arms of Chandon and sympathetic Dutch officials. They were all given transport to Paramaribo and then to Georgetown, British Guiana. All but six went on to fight for De Gaulle in Africa.

When news of this escape reached Cayenne, the pro-Vichy officials went wild with rage and stepped up security in St. Laurent. Any escape to Albina was now considered an attempt to join the Free French and was punishable by death. The six in Georgetown, who for reasons of age were not permitted to go on to Africa, were sent back to Guiana to face charges of treason. All condemned to death, they were never executed, but spent two years in solitary confinement before being pardoned after the war.

By 1943 tension had risen in the colony and though most in Guiana were content to "blow with the wind" when it came to politics, a general feeling of discontent was becoming evident as the measures taken by the Vichy authorities became more and more repressive.

Tension gave way to absurdity with a very serious twist when it came to portraits. Francis Lagrange, a convict sent to the bagne for art forgery and counterfeiting, was commissioned by one of the career officials to paint a series of portraits of Petain to be hung behind his desk as proof of his allegiance to Vichy in face of higher officials.

Lagrange did the work as ordered and scenes of Petain in full uniform were hung behind the desk of this official. Yet who could tell? A few days later this official called Lagrange back to his office: he was taking no chances. He removed the large painting of Petain from the wall and handed it back to Lagrange. Only finished the day before, the paint was still fresh.

"You don't want the picture, sir?"

"Of course I want the picture, it's a splendid representation of our greatest man. However, France is fecund. There are several great men on the scene today...Lagrange, I would like you to paint on the other side of this portrait an equally magnificent likeness of France's second greatest man."

"Of course you are referring to General De Gaulle?"

"Of course, Lagrange. Do you think you can have this picture back for me by tonight?"

"I'll do my best, sir."

"I thought you would, Lagrange. It is easier to have one portrait to cover all emergencies than to have to mess about with several of them. One never knows when the wrong portrait will pop up. This way we simply turn the picture over, depending on the circumstances. I am a patriotic citizen of the Republic, Lagrange. I am loyal to the nation, not to any one man. I would not want my patriotism to be misunderstood."

The devastation continued in the convict and relégué camps and the Vichy officials remained unmoved. During an inspection tour of the bagne, the Vichy governor, noted many injuries among the convicts and held the injured men responsible stating in his report, "certain individuals prefer to wound themselves to the point of requiring amputation than to submit to obligatory labor."

The repression increased. Charles Pean of the Salvation Army was put into detention and then ordered out of the colony for subversive activities. Suspected civilian opponents of Petain were rounded up and interned on the islands.

There was one exception. Soon after the fall of France, the authorities in Cayenne received a telegram from Vichy, the implication of which could not be misunderstood. It read, "Requested urgently for armistice committee a list of all convicts and relégués of the German Reich with exact reasons for conviction and details of crime. Stop."

The A.P. sent a list of over one hundred Germans, Austrians, Poles Belgians, Czechs, etc. Soon after, the names of several dozen were returned by cable and pardons were granted to them. Among the Germans was Otto Klems, known as the "German Lawrence of Arabia." He joined the French Foreign Legion in 1922 and was rapidly promoted in rank after seeing combat against rebel forces in French

Morocco. A first-rate soldier, he nonetheless deserted and roamed the countryside where he learned to speak several local dialects. Eventually he met up with rebel forces and offered his services to them. Soon this ex-Foreign Legionaire was chief of staff of the rebel forces of Abd El Krim. Later captured in an ambush, he was sentenced to death but his sentence was reduced to hard labor for life by the intervention of the German government in 1927.

By 1943, with the U.S. Army constructing an airbase outside of Cayenne, French Guiana was pushed into the De Gaulle camp. Inspired by Felix Eboué, who was born in Cayenne and who was in the forefront of Free French forces in Chad, pressure began to mount. Governor Veber could no longer hold his position when the allies invaded North Africa.

Representatives of Brazil and the U.S. were in touch with Cayenne's mayor Ulrich Sophie and leaders of the local Free French faction. By March 1943 war ships of Brazil and the U.S. were off the Guiana coast and on the 17th Veber publicly accepted a change-over to a pro-De Gaulle regime. He had been associated for too long with Petain and it was too late for him to change sides. He was permitted to leave the colony and was placed under surveillance by American officials when he arrived in Puerto Rico.

The next day American and Brazilian naval officers from the offshore fleet arrived in Cayenne and were given an enthusiastic reception by the town's populace. Those who had been most outspoken for Petain were now long-time De Gaulle supporters and overnight all who could still change sides, did. And the official with the double portrait didn't forget to turn it over.

Just as quickly a power struggle developed. When hearing of Guiana's change, De Gaulle in London and Giraud in Algeria simultaneously sent governors to Cayenne. The first to arrive would assume power. On March 26, 1943 Jean Rapenne, the Giraud candidate, beat the De Gaulle candidate by twenty-four hours and took power as governor. The distinction between De Gaulle and Giraud wasn't well understood by residents of Cayenne who came out to greet him. To their cries of "Vive De Gaulle" Rapenne shouted just as enthusiastically, "Vive Giraud." During his eighteen months as governor, Rapenne had absolute power since the elected positions in the colony had been suspended during the Vichy regime.

The War had taken its toll. Only half as many men were alive in the bagne in 1944 as were in 1940. Over 2,000 had died as a result of privation caused by the Atlantic blockade which cut off food and medicine.

There was no longer any question of sending relégués to Guiana when the war ended and in 1945, the provisional government in Paris set in motion plans to liquidate the penal colony and bring all the prisoners back to France. Dr. Xavier Sainz was appointed Director of the penal administration and head of the liquidation committee. His mission was twofold, as he would also be responsible for bringing back to health convicts devastated by the war. Some were down to one hundred pounds, more from the lack of drugs to combat tropical diseases than from the lack of food.

The liquidation was not going to be a small job either. It would take time, since the lifeblood of the colony couldn't be extracted overnight. The bagne had lasted nearly a century and all of Guiana was tied in one way or another with the prison. Its closure was not about to be well received by those who had benefited from it.

Most in Guiana didn't want the bagne to end either. The convicts had provided a virtually free labor force. Who would clean the streets and the open sewers now?

Just after the war, the jungle camps were closed and the islands abandoned. Only the camp in St. Laurent was in full operation as the entire structure of the penal colony began to crumble — those who remained were not closely guarded and most wandered around in the streets during the day.

The exact number of libérés could not be determined since doublage had been abolished and no one reported to the police. The Salvation Army was called back to the colony and Charles Pean took up the job of he had started before the war. Since the post-war period left few ships available, it would take years to ship all the convicts to France.

Convicts still under sentence could apply to the Ministry of Justice for pardons. Of course, pardons were granted according to the severity of the original sentence and the amount of time already served. Those under life sentence would have the hardest time obtaining liberation. The stone walls of French jails were nothing to look forward to. Still, the atmosphere had changed. Many would be going home after twenty, sometimes thirty years in Guiana.

In the streets of Cayenne and St. Laurent, the closing of the bagne was being felt. Some businesses had gone under, since there were no longer guards and prison officials to pour money into the economy. The reality began to set in that without the penal colony Guiana would die.

The liquidation continued in typical Guiana style: as each camp closed, the jungle moved in. What had been a thriving penal colony was now leaving and turning St. Laurent into a ghost town. Looting of prison supplies was rampant and certain officials made fortunes in the confusion. This would be the last racket in Guiana and everyone wanted to get in on it.

By the end of 1946 the repatriation was in full swing and every mail-boat carried a few dozen prisoners back to France. Lack of funds now deterred few, since the government was willing to pay three-quarters of the fare and the balance was less than one hundred francs. The Salvation Army paid that amount if a man was flat broke.

In the spring of 1947, French Guiana's status changed from colony to department. Little was expected from this change and little did actually change. Responsibility for liquidation was passed to the Interior Ministry. Some of the officials left and new ones arrived with different titles. It was becoming clear that this new department would soon regress to the state of the colony in 1852, just after the abolition of slavery.

On June 28, 1947 the last 600 prisoners at St. Laurent were set free. Just as simply as that. The prison gates were opened and the men spilled out into the streets of the town. Lucien Bellouard was "liberated" at this time.

"We all headed out into the streets," he recalled. "Nobody knew where they would sleep that night as the guards just yelled that it was no longer their problem. By night we filled every back alley of St. Laurent and most of us slept in the public market. The only reason they let us out was that it cost them too much to keep us inside."

Though officially closed, the bagne lived on as the Salvation Army continued to ship convicts back to France until as late as 1952. And they tried to help former prisoners in France find jobs.

During the 1950s, French Guiana sank into a severe depression and survived only by the grace of French subsidies. As it does to this day.

But the bagne was not and is not over. It didn't end for the more than 300 former prisoners who refused to return to France and for the convicts who had contracted leprosy.

A few were able to establish themselves in small businesses and one or two did quite well. For most, it was the same story of tafia and vagabondage. No one paid much attention to them; they were a common sight in the gutters. At the beginning of 1988 fewer than ten were still alive in French Guiana.

COLONY OF THE DAMNED

The midday silence in Cayenne is broken only by a distant radio thumping out the sounds of Madonna. Walking from the better part of town to the slums takes only several minutes while the lyrics play softly from every fifth house. The town is asleep.

Near the creek where the Brazilian sail-boats arrive carrying clandestine workers and contraband, there is a man lying in the gutter. At a distance he seems young and well-built, but on closer inspection it turns out that he's well past eighty. Newspapers cover his face; an old rice sack is his pillow and mattress.

His face is deeply lined. The tattoos that cover his body have faded. His ankles and feet are swollen and are covered with white patches. He has leprosy.

Henri Laurette has little to say these days. The tafia he drinks from dawn to dusk won't bring back his youth. The treatments at the hospital won't stop his skin from rotting to the bone.

But he is not alone. Down the street, emerging from a new and spotless home, is Cayenne's most successful physician. He is in a hurry to get to the hospital to see his patients — but not in that much of a hurry, for he stops at the spot where Henri lies. Though the reek of alcohol hits him yards away, he approaches. He strokes the old man's head with one hand and with his other slips a few francs into Henri's claw-like hand.

They have known each other for thirty-five years. When the doctor was a youth, Henri was there. When the doctor was eighteen and left to go to Paris, Henri was there. When he returned to Cayenne ten years later with his wife and children, Henri was still in the same spot. He hadn't budged.

The coins slip out and fall to the ground. Henri's eyes glisten as if he is fighting back tears. The trembling of an old drunkard's fingers? He nods to the bottle of tafia by his feet and grins. The doctor grins as well. They share their private joke.

But they are lying to each other. Losing his grip has nothing to do with the vile rum that Henri belts back at all hours. His hands are losing sensation and turning into stumps; it is common with advancing leprosy.

The defeat on Henri's face is nothing the doctor can cure. He knows that and moves on, not wishing to cause Henri any more humiliation.

Henri Laurette is no longer much of a man, but the little he has left, his hands, are slowly being eaten away. Throughout his life Laurette has lived by his hands. As a young sailor with the French Navy, those hands wrestled and tamed the anaconda-like cables on many ships decks, bringing notice from the officers and promotion in rank.

But those hands were his downfall as well, as over fifty years ago they calmly broke the neck of the total stranger he found in his bed. The hands that tightened around the throat and choked the life out of the only woman he had ever loved, to stop her from screaming when she saw what Laurette had done to the lover who lay naked at the foot of the bed with his tongue protruding.

Those hands had slapped at millions of mosquitos in the swamps of Guiana and had worked to cut down thousands of trees which the guards left to rot at the jungle. Those hands, Laurette knows, are beginning to look like the decaying timber.

Perhaps the most vengeful among us will see Laurette's end as a sort of poetic justice, the hands of the strangler turning into the claws of a leper.

Henri Laurette takes another swig from his bottle and tries to forget.

If you look hard enough in Cayenne and St. Laurent, you'll find the last men of Devil's Island. A few here, a few there, and in the St. Laurent hospital maybe half a dozen. On the streets several remain, clutching bottles of tafia. To them, the hospital and the retirement home are just different types of prisons and they have had enough of prison. Out on the streets they can live out their last days in some semblance of freedom.

Consider the thousands who came to Guiana as convicts. Each year there are fewer and fewer vieux blancs and probably in five years time there will be none left. The occasional traveller to French Guiana will be told that there are none left now, since the bagne is somewhat of a taboo subject in Cayenne, though in St. Laurent traces of the prisons are everywhere and cannot be hidden. Lacking the grace to disappear in the jungle like many of the forest camps, the main penitentiary in St. Laurent still stands and is inhabited by squatters.

The jungle camps have been eaten up by dense vegetation, but they can be uncovered by hacking through the dense bush with a machete. A few reminders of the prison can be found in the ruins of the barracks, bits of kerosene lamps and iron bars that have almost turned to powder. And there are bricks with the letters "A.P." stamped on them, scattered everywhere within the vicinity of the jungle camps.

Deserted at the end of World War II, the islands were left to rot. Some years ago on Royale the guards' mess hall was converted into a restaurant and hotel for tourists. The rest of the island is littered with rotting buildings and workshops from the prison era. The Islands are now property of the Guiana Space Center.

St. Joseph is much less tourist-trodden than Royale, and only recently have small groups of French Foreign Legionnaires begun to use the island as a weekend retreat from the rigors of army life on the mainland. A minute's walk from the sunbathing soldiers, the reclusion cells jut out. Half structure, half vegetation, their wooden doors have completely disintegrated in the humidity and the corrugated iron roof is long gone. Only the cement walls and rusting ceiling bars remain.

Lastly, there is Devil's Island. Hardly anyone sets foot on that island today — it's much too dangerous to land on. Years ago it was described as so small that one could circle the island while smoking a cigarette. These days it takes much longer since the neat paths maintained years ago have vanished.

Dreyfus' hut, or what decayed stones remain from it, is perched on a slight elevation at the center of the island. From there you can watch the waves pound endlessly onto the shore. Those who frequent the islands nowadays claim that the sharks who used to swim in great numbers offshore have disappeared because there are no longer any convict corpses to eat.

There are few accessible parts of French Guiana that were not touched by the penal colony. Between St. Laurent and St. Jean, traces of the old prison centers are visible from Maroni's bank. The tracks go right into the river across from the old leper island. St. Louis is, of course, now deserted, but one still finds the same "A.P." bricks and corrugated iron as in the jungle camps. The convict lepers were long ago transferred to the civilian leper colony at Acarouany. Those who didn't go ended up on the streets, since most lepers weren't permitted to return to France after liquidation as they couldn't pass a health examination that declared them "non-contagious."

Some scenery masks the past. Where the road building camp at Kourou once stood, a luxury hotel was built to house technician from France who come to work at the rocket-launching pad nearby. At night along its dark and deserted beach, quite a few people have felt fearfully uneasy for no apparent reason. Old Creoles attribute this to ghosts, for according to local belief, the place and circumstance of death play an important part in the manifestation of the spirit, and there are many convict corpses in the vicinity from Route Zero.

Without any real interest in preserving the last remaining prison structures, local politicians have debated over the years about demolishing what is left. They are a source of curiosity for some, embarrassment for others. With the only historical past of any significance being prison and confinement, the locals are reluctant to dwell on it. The outside world knows French Guiana for Dreyfus and Papillon — not an enviable legacy.

In France, most of the repatriated former prisoners are long dead. A small number live out their final days in obscurity — mostly in retirement homes or on the streets. A few among them have been convicted of new crimes and will die in jail. In 1975, eighty-five year old Charles Bouchet who spent twenty-seven years in Guiana for manslaughter was in jail again. He had been charged with the stabbing death of a rival of his own age in a Paris old-age home. And there are still a number of escaped convicts scattered throughout Latin America.

What remains in French Guiana as a result of a century of convict labor? The answer is — nothing.

Since the closing of the prisons, almost the entire local population has gone to Cayenne where government jobs are abundant. The few efforts to start farms in the interior have fallen aside. Every year the trade deficit grows and is absorbed by France. And every year Guiana grows more dependent than ever on France.

And after 300 years of French rule, Guiana still looks to Paris for a solution to all this.

In 1975, Paris proposed to send 30,000 French settlers to Guiana. It was felt that these new colonists would develop the interior and make the territory self-sufficient. Dubbed "The Green Plan," new settlers began arriving and in a few short months over 3,000 were in Cayenne.

But nothing had been done to prepare for these colonists. Because of bureaucratic errors they had to wait months to get their parcel of land and many took to sitting in Cayenne bars where they rapidly drank away their savings. Most were quickly discouraged and returned to France. Only a handful actually started farms in the interior and those few left after several months to look for desk jobs in Cayenne. No lessons were learned from the 1763 Kourou expedition, and the latest of French Guiana's development plans was quickly forgotten.

The most recent colonists in French Guiana have been Mhong tribesmen forced to leave their homeland by the war in Indochina. For these Laotian refugees, French Guiana seemed like the ideal place. Finding few countries willing to take them in the late 1970s, France sent two transports. The Mhongs quickly cleared jungle and planted crops, creating two new villages.

But young Mhongs have begun to make trips to Cayenne. They see how the rest of the population lives, and a number have started to look for work in the capital. Who can blame them? Government jobs and subsidies have artificially pumped up the standard of living to the highest in South America.

When the Mhongs first arrived, there was some local opposition to their implantation. Some feared continued Mhong immigration out of fear that unchecked Mhongs would soon be the largest ethnic group in French Guiana. The project was scaled down and the number of new Mhong arrivals was reduced.

Their economic effect has been positive. Before their arrival, fresh fruit and vegetables had to be imported from France as local production didn't satisfy French Guiana's needs. The Mhongs have been able to reduce this dependence, though local vendors still sell produce air-freighted from Europe. The cost of living in French Guiana is the highest of any French département. Tomatos sell for four dollars a pound in the local market.

In a sense, some of the horror of the bagne continues. The drama of escaped men hunted through the jungle and of road construction in the swamps goes on. The Kourou Space Center is guarded by the French Foreign Legion, since the rocket launching pad is a most vulnerable target for terrorists.

It is the Foreign Legion which is building the highway to St. Georges through the thickest mangrove and jungle. An eventual coastal road link between Cayenne and the Brazilian border, planned a century ago, is still years from completion — but already several monuments honoring Legionnaires who have died on this project dot the trail. Even with bulldozers and helicopters the spector of Route Zero remains.

Every once in a while a deserter emerges from the bush, half crazed and on the verge of death. After a spell in the hospital, the court-martial inquiry takes down the tragic recital of a man driven to the brink of suicide in seventy-two hours. And that's all the time it takes to crack when you are without food, devoured by the mosquitos and completely lost in the swamps. The terror never really leaves you.

The last few years have seen a dramatic increase in expenditures from Paris to keep Guiana functioning and Cayenne has, in some respects, the air of a wealthy town. New cars and luxury items are everywhere and almost all of it can be linked directly or indirectly to public sector financing.

Perhaps this is what France wants. A French Guiana totally dependent on France would be reluctant to move for independence. An important reason for bringing the space center to Kourou was Algeria gaining independence, and the loss of Guiana, hence the loss of Kourou, would be a strategic disaster for France. As well, French Guiana's statute of département *Outre-Mer* confers identical rights to inhabitants of Guiana. It can be roughly compared to the status of Alaska and Hawaii and many (though not all) French Guianese consider themselves loyal citizens of the French Republic. On the other hand, a minority who favor independence want the French out.

From a strange quarter in Guiana has come admiration for one of the policies of Francois Mitterand. The 1981 abolition of capital punishment in France was applauded by all of the former convicts in Cayenne and St. Laurent. When a man has seen one of his comrades publicly guillotined, the sight never leaves him. The split second when the knife cuts and the blood spurts is an image that never is forgotten. To them, the very perversion of the act and the system that sanctions it are equally reprehensible. As the old prison saying goes, "Justice is made, crime for crime."

But then, these men are criminals.

Since the abolition of the death penalty, debate has started up again in France on what to do with long-term convicts. Whether repressive or humanitarian, most of the projects tried in the last several years have met with mixed results. There has also been talk of resuming transportation. Will anyone look at Guiana and its lessons before the first convoy leaves on its way to a forgotten corner of the French Empire, overlooked during de-colonization?

Another irony is that criminals sentenced to long prison terms for crimes committed in French Guiana are now normally transferred to France, since the département doesn't have space to keep them. The road is reversed; it is now Frenchmen from France who commit the most violent crimes in Guiana. Many arrive in Cayenne without work or desert from the French Foreign Legion; some have come in a sort of unofficial exile after scrapes with the law in France.

For nearly a century St. Laurent was host to France's most depraved criminals. In December 1987 several young men were arrested in the largest case of mass murder in French criminal history, involving the strangulation of at least twenty-six old women in Paris. Twenty-two year-old Jean-Theirry Mathurin, born in St. Larent du Maroni, was taken into detention to await trial for his part in the killings. Somewhere there is a moral in this.

At the time of this writing, a last-ditch effort is underway in Guiana to preserve and restore some of the remaining prison buildings on the Iles du Salut and in St. Laurent. The thought is that Guiana's reputation might improve if the past is put into perspective. And it makes sense as there is little reason to associate Guiana's past prison reputation with the present. On the contrary, one only has to look to the Guiana Space Center in Kourou. The success of Europe's *Ariane* satellite launcher has begun to change French Guiana's image.

But a bad reputation dies hard. During a recent trip to New York, the author stopped at Air France's Fifth Avenue office to inquire about fare changes to French Guiana. At the mention of Cayenne, the smile vanished from the face of the pretty Parisian reservationist. She recoiled in horror. "Monsieur," she murmured, "why would you want to go there? *C'est le bagne!*"

AFTERWORD

In April 1987, Lucien Bellouard died at the age of ninety-five, disgusted at having to spend his last days at the squalid former prison hospital in St. Laurent.

The St. Laurent known to Henri Bauve, Lucien Bellouard and the dozen other survivors of the penal colony has changed in the last several years. After a few years of stability, neighboring Surinam's civilian government was overthrown in a military coup in 1980. In 1982, army sergeant Desi Bouterse seized control and took over the military junta. A brief flirtation with Fidel Castro ended after the U.S. invasion of Grenada began a fear that Surinam was next. Internal problems increased as the Paramaribo-based government quickly alienated the bush-negro population of the Maroni and by 1986 an active rebellion developed in the region. Called "Jungle Commandos," their leader Roni Brunswick has effectively cut Surinam in half. In September 1986, the road link between Surinam and French Guiana was cut and Albina evacuated. For the first time since the closing of the bagne, the Maroni river in the vicinity of St. Laurent was heavily guarded and identity checks again became the order of the day. Bush-negro and Indian refugees began to trickle into French Guiana, since attacks on river villages by the Surinam army and the rebels have completely disrupted life on the river.

195

France has accepted these refugees and several camps have been set up in the St. Laurent area. Charvein, completely lost in jungle overgrowth after the end of the bagne, was recently cleared to build another refugee camp. The refugee population in January 1988 was 10,000 at the moment of Surinam's return to civilian rule. The hope is that these refugees will return quickly to the other side of the river. This is a delicate problem for France, since these refugees now represent ten percent of French Guiana's population. Should they stay, the ethnic balance of French Guiana will change dramatically which will have potential disruptive effects on local politics.

These events fell at a bad time, when representatives of Club Med visited French Guiana in September 1986 and expressed interest in turning the Camp de la Transportation in St. Laurent into a resort. Though government officials state that "the plan will progress," the old prison is still rotting and inhabited by squatters.

SELECTED BIBLIOGRAPHY

BOOKS

Alexakis, Chantal. *Les Bagnes*. Paris: Pygmalion, 1979.

Allison-Booth, William E. *Devil's Island: Revelations of the French Penal Settlements in Guiana*. New York: Putnam, 1931.

Andouard, Jacques. *Roi de L'Evasion*. Paris: Alsatia, 1962.

Anquetil, Georges. *Un cas typique des conséquences de la fraude électorale aux colonies. La France peut perdre sa plus vieille et sa plus riche colonie d'Amérique, la Guyane*. Paris: Imprimerie Parisiennes reunies, 1928.

Aubert, Michel. *Paradis en Enfer*. Paris: Robert Laffont, 1972.

Batzler-Heim, Georg. *Horrors of Cayenne*. New York: R. Smith, 1930.

Belbenoit, René. *Dry Guillotine*. New York: E.P. Dutton, 1938.
— *Hell on Trial*. New York: E.P. Dutton, 1940.

Bernede, Arthur. *L'Affaire Bougrat*. Paris: Tallandier, 1933.

Bonny, Jacques. *Mon père, l'inspecteur Bonny*. Paris: Laffont, 1975.

Boucly, Jean. *De la transportation des condamnés aux travaux forcés*. Dijon: 1932.

Bourdet-Pleville, Michel. *Des galériens, des forçats et des bagnards*. Paris: Plon, 1957.

Brasseur, Gérard. *La Guyane Française: Un bilan de trente années*. Paris: La documentation française, 1978.

Bredin, Jean-Denis. *L'Affaire*. Paris: Julliard, 1983.

Brousseau, Georges. *Les Richesses de la Guyane Française*. Paris: Société d'éditions scientifiques, 1901.

Calloch, J.M. *La mort au ralenti*. Paris: Menges, 1979.

Casey, Daniel. *Guyane*. Paris: Schlaber, 1889.

Cendrars, Blaise. *Rhum*. Paris: Grasset, 1930.

Cerfberr, A.E. *La Guyane*. Paris: Adolphe Delehays, 1854.

Charrière, Henri. *Papillon*. Paris: Robert Laffont, 1969.
— *Banco*. Paris: Robert Laffont, 1972.

Connell, Evan S. *Son of the Morning Star*. San Francisco: North Point Press, 1984.

Danan, A. *Cayenne*. Paris: Fayard, 1934.

Dangoise, Arthur. *Guyane Française*. Paris: Roberge, 1909.

Darlix, Paul. *Avec les "durs" de Cayenne à Caracas*. Paris: Baudinière, 1932.

Delpeche, René. *Parmi les fauves et les requins*. Paris: d'Hallium, 1955.

Destrem, Michel. *Le dossier d'un déporté de 1804*. Paris: Georges Bellais, 1904.

Devèze, Michel. *Cayenne*. Paris: Julliard, 1965.
— *Les Guyanes*. Paris: Presses Universitaires de France, 1968.

Dieudonné, Eugène. *La vie des forçats*. Paris: Gallimard, 1930.

Deuel, John Vanderveer. *White Cayuca*. Boston: Houghton Mifflin, 1934.

Dupont-Gonin, Pierre. *La Guyane Française*. Geneva: Droz, 1970.

Dhur, Jacques. *Visions du bagne.* Paris: Ferenczi, 1925.

Dreyfus, Alfred. *Cinq années de ma vie, 1894-1899.* (reprint of the 1901 edition) Paris: Fasquelle, 1962.

Ettinghoffer, Paul Colestin. *The Island of the Doomed.* New York, 1935.

Falcionelli, Albert. *Les Sociétés secrètes italiennes.* Paris: Payot, 1936.

Fenigre, Jean. *Guyane Française. De la transportation et des établissements pénitenciers.* Lille: Bayart, 1864.

Findlay, D.G.A. *De geschiedenis van het bagno van Frans Guyana.*

Flotat, Roger. *Au plus chaud de l'enfer du bagne.* Paris: Scorpion, 1957.

Franceschi, A. *De l'organisation locale de la transportation.* Laval: E. Jamin, 1895.

Franck, Harry. *Working North from Patagonia.* New York: Century, 1921.

Galmot, Jean. *Un mort vivait parmi nous.* Paris: Littré, 1922.

Guillebaud, J.C. *Les confetti de l'empire.* Paris: Seuil, 1976.

Halliburton, Richard. *New Worlds to Conquer.* Indianapolis: Bobbs Merrill, 1929.

Hamel, Ian. *Les Guyanais: Français en sursis?* Paris: Entente, 1979.

Hassoldt-Davis. *The Jungle and the Damned.* Boston: Little Brown, 1952.

Henry, Dr. Arthur. *Guyane Française: Capitale Cayenne.* Paris: Gallimard, 1935.

— *La Guyane Française, son histoire, 1604-1946.* (reprint of 1951) Cayenne: le mayouri, 1981.

Hess, A. *A l'Ile du Diable.* Paris: P. Lamm, 1898.

Hurault, Jean-Marcel. *Français et Indiens en Guyane.* Paris: 10/18, 1972.

Hue, Fernand. *La Guyane Française.* Paris: Lecène, 1886.

Henri, Edmond. *Etude critique de la transportation.* Paris: Larose, 1912.

Krarup-Nielsen, Aage H. *Hell Beyond the Seas.* Garden City, NY: Garden City Publishing Co., 1938.

Lamothe, A. *Mémoires d'un déporté à la Guyane Française.* Paris: A. Josse, 1859.

Larique, M. *Dans la brousse.* Paris: Gallimard, 1933.

Lacroix, Louis. *Les derniers voyages de forçats et de voiliers en Guyane.* Paris: Editions Maritimes et d'Outre-mer, 1970.

Laporte, Paul. *La Guyane des Ecoles.* Paris: A. Corps, 1915.

Lagrange, Francis with William Murray. *Flag on Devil's Island.* Garden City, NY: Doubleday, 1961.

Le Boucher, L. *Ce qu'il faut connaître du bagne.* Paris: Boivin, 1930.

Le Clère, Marcel. *La vie quotidienne dans les bagnes.* Paris: Hachette, 1973.

Lewis, David L. *Prisoners of Honor: The Dreyfus Affair.* New York: William Morrow, 1973.

Londres, Albert. *Au bagne.* Paris: Albin Michel, 1924.

Mesclon, A. *Comment j'ai subi quinze ans de bagne.* Paris: 1924.

Maroger, M. *Bagne.* Paris: Denoël, 1937. (Attacked in France for slander against prison officials).

Michelot, Jean-Claude. *La guillotine sèche.* Paris: Fayard, 1981. (Also knew Henri Bauve and Lucien Bellouard.)

Miles, William F.S. *Elections and Ethnicity in French Martinique.* New York: Praeger, 1986.

Mury, Paul. *Les Jésuites à Cayenne.* Strasbourg: Le Roux, 1895.

Nordhoff, Charles and James Hall. *Men Without Country.* Boston: Little Brown, 1942. (Made into the film *Passage to Marseille* .)

Niles, Blair. *Condemned to Devil's Island.* New York: Harcourt Brace, 1928. (Made into the film *Condemned*).
— *Free.* New York: Harcourt Brace, 1930.

Pean, Charles. *Terre de Bagne.* Paris: Atlis, 1933.

Pierre, Michel. *La terre de la grande punition.* Paris: Ramsay, 1982.

Pedrick, Dad. *Jungle Gold.* Indianapolis: Bobbs Merrill, 1930.

Poli, François, *Gentlemen Bagnards.* Paris: Presses de la Cité, 1959.

Quris, Bernard. *Les portes de l'enfer.* Paris: France-Empire, 1975.

Rickards, Colin. *The Man from Devil's Island.* New York: Stein & Day, 1968.

Rousseau, Dr. Louis. *Un médecin au bagne.* Paris: Fleury, 1930.

Roussenq, Paul. *L'enfer du bagne.* Vichy: Pucheux, 1957.

Sable, Victor. *La transformation des iles d'Amériques en département françaises.* Paris: Larose, 1955.

Sale, Richard. *Not too Narrow...Not too Deep.* New York: Simon & Schuster, 1936. (Made into the film *Strange Passage* .)

Schwarzbeck, Frank. *Französisch Guiana.* Heidelberg: Esprint, 1982.

Seaton, George. *Isle of the Damned.* New York: Farrar Straus, 1951.

Sinclair, Gordon. *Loose Among Devils.* New York: Farrar Straus, 1935.

Sophie, Ulrich. *Le ralliement de la Guyane Française à la France Libre.* Paris: Soulanges, 1964.

Thomas, Bernard. *Jacob.* Paris: Tchou, 1970.

Thésée, Françoise. *Un mémoire inédit de Victor Hugues sur la Guyane.* Paris: Paul Geunthner, 1970.

Vaudé, Raymond. *Matricule 52.306.* Paris: Les débats de l'histoire, 1972.

Vignon, Robert. *Guyane d'aujourd'hui et de demain.* Cayenne: Imprimerie Paul Laporte, 1952.

Villiers, Gérard de. *Papillon Epinglé.* Paris: Presses de la Cité, 1970.

Willis, William. *Damned and Damned Again.* New York: St. Martins, 1959.

Wright, Gordon. *Between the Guillotine and Liberty.* New York: Oxford University Press, 1983.

Zaccone, Pierre. *Histoire des bagnes.* Clichy: Paul Dupont.

ARTICLES

Ballof, Daniel. *Bagnards indochinois en Guyane.*

Blin, Dr. G. *Sur l'ankylostomiase dans l'élément pénal de la Guyane.* Annales d'Hygiène et de Médecine coloniale. 1914, Vol. 17, p. 179.

— *L'uncinariose chez les chercheurs d'or et les forçats du Maroni.* Annales d'Hygiène et de Médecine coloniale. 1914, Vol. 17, p. 149.

Drekonja-Kornat, Gerhard. *On the Edge of Civilization.* Caribbean Review. 1984, Vol. 13, #2, p. 26.

Floch, Dr. Hervé. *La lèpre au bagne guyanais. Son évolution durant un siècle (1852-1950). Ses particularités.* International Journal of Leprosy. 1951, Vol. 19, #3, p. 283.

Floch, Dr. Hervé and Dr. Pierre Destombes. *Revue, à la disparition du bagne, de l'évolution du comportement de l'élément pénal devant l'endémie lépreuse en Guyane.* Publication de l'Institut Pasteur de la Guyane et du territoire de l'Inini. 1950, # 222.

Gritzner, Charles F. *French Guiana: Development Trends in Post-Prison Era.* The Journal of Geography. Vol. 62, #4, 1962.

— *French Guiana Penal Colony: Its Role in Colonial Development.* The Journal of Geography. Vol. 63, #7, 1964.

Lacroix, Jean-Paul. *L'Affaire Seznec.* Paris-Jour. 1978, #5.

Leger, Dr. Marcel. *Parasitisme intestinal à la Guyane Française dans la population locale et dans l'élément pénal.* Bulletin de la Société de Pathologie Exotique. 1917, Vol. 10, p. 557.

— *La lèpre à la Guyane Française dans l'élément pénal.* Bulletin de la Société de Pathologie Exotique. 1918, Vol. 11, p. 793.

Miles, Alexander and Colin Rickards. *Shackles to Satellites: How Europe Hopes to Beat the Americans at Their Own Game.* Caribbean Business News. January, 1980, cover story.

Orgeas, Dr. Jean. *La colonisation de la Guyane par la transportation.* Archives de médecine navale. 1883. Vol. 39, p. 161, 241, 321.

Rousseau, Dr. Louis. *Faillite morale et utilitaire de la transportation en Guyane: Etat sanitaire général de la Colonie pénitentiaire.* Académie des Sciences Coloniales; compterendus des séances - communications. Vol. 2, 1925.

Smith, Richard, *The Man Who Broke Into Devil's Island!* Argosy, April, 1974.

Schwarzbeck, Frank. *Recycling a Forgotten Colony.* Caribbean Review. 1984, Vol. 13, #2, p. 23.

Vignon, Robert. *French Guiana: Looking Ahead.* Caribbean Commission Monthly Bulletin, June 1954, #251.

OFFICIAL DOCUMENTS

Convention pour l'exécution du transport des relégués et condamnés de France à la Guyane. Ministère des Colonies, Service de la Marine marchande, contrat du 12 avril 1921. (Contract between French Ministry of Colonies and Compagnie Nantaise de Navigation à vapeur for convict transport).

Rapport fait au nom de la commission de la législation civile et criminelle chargée d'examiner le projet de la loi portant réforme de la peine des travaux forcés et du régime de la rélegation et suppression de la transportation à la Guyane, par Gaston Monnerville, Député. Chambre des Députés, session de 1937, annexe au procès-verbal de la séance du 20 juin 1937. (Legislative proposal to abolish Guiana penal colony).

ARCHIVES

Archives départementales de la Guyane
Cayenne, French Guiana

Archives Nationales (Centre des Archives d'Outre-Mer)
Aix-en-Provence, France

OTHER SOURCES

The New York Times
Caribbean Business News
Information Caraibe

In 1979 the author found documents discarded by the *Administration Pénitentiaire* and left rotting and rat-eaten for thirty years in the St. Laurent prison. Included: convicts' dossiers, escape interrogations, libéré I.D. booklets, letters written by convicts to prison officials, etc. It was not until 1983 that a formal archives service was created in French Guiana.